Caroli

"Caroline Fei-Yeng Kwok's narrative

the experiences and perspective of a Chinese immigrant to Canada from Hong Kong labelled as having manic-depression. Equally impressive is the fact that this beautiful book is written in a poetic manner with great depth and insight about madness by one who knows it from within. It will appeal to a wide audience including people with a psychiatric history as well as people who work with them and anyone interested in cross-cultural experiences of the mental health system in Canada."

Geoffrey Reaume, Assistant Professor,
Critical Disability Studies, York University, Toronto

⟷

"*Free To Fly* is a harrowing yet ultimately uplifting account of one Chinese-Canadian woman's odyssey from despair to hope. Stricken with manic-depression, Caroline Kwok has to learn to cope with not only the ordeal of involuntary confinement and the authoritarianism of the medical profession, but also with the social stigma that attaches to mental illness and the uncomprehending attitudes of her family and ethnic community. Her moving and inspiring narative will appeal to fellow sufferers and health -care professionals as well as to general readers, many of whom have little idea of what life looks like from the inside of a mental hospital."

Greig Henderson, Assoc. Prof, Dept. of English, University of Toronto

⟷

"This book is a testament to the persistence of Caroline Kwok, who has struggled to deal with the impact of her manic depression to work and life. Writing openly about such distressing changes in her life, she gives the readers the opportunity to share first-hand in the uniqueness of her suffering. Her words reveal a world of torment and passion. This is a story worth reading."

Dr. Ronald Ruskin, Staff Psychiatrist, Mount Sinai Hospital, Toronto,
M.D., F.R.C.P (C), Dip. Psych., Canada

⟷

"Caroline has courageously shared some of the most vulnerable moments from the extreme spectrum of an often intolerable human condition. A precious reminder to any sufferer that they are not alone."

Jane Lowry, writer and survivor

⟷

"This is a compelling account of one's struggle through manic-depression and its long road to recovery. This book will help motivate others to find creative ways to deal with stresses and recover one's health."

Martha Ocampo, Director, Across Boundaries

Free to Fly

A Story of Manic Depression

Caroline Fei-Yeng Kwok

foreword by **Dr. Mary V. Seeman, O.C., MDCM**

Inclusion Press

Library and Archives Canada Cataloguing in Publication

Kwok, Caroline Fei-Yeng, 1951-

Free to fly : a story of manic-depression / by Caroline Fei-Yeng Kwok ; foreword by Mary Seeman.

Previously published under title: The tormented mind.
Includes bibliographical references.

ISBN-13: 978-1-895418-72-9
ISBN-10: 1-895418-72-0

1. Kwok, Caroline Fei-Yeng, 1951- --Mental health. 2. Manic-depressive persons--Canada--Biography. 3. Manic-depressive illness--Treatment. I. Kwok, Caroline Fei-Yeng, 1951- . Tormented mind. II. Title.

RC516.K86 2006 616.89'50092 C2006-904251-9

Inclusion Press

24 Thome Crescent • Toronto, Ontario • M6H 2S5 • Canada

416-658-5363 FAX 416-658-5067

inclusionpress@inclusion.com

www.inclusion.com

Table of Contents

PART THREE

PART FOUR

PART FIVE

To

Dr. Richard Selzer
of
Yale University

and

In Loving Memory
of
my parents

Woon-Lum Kwok
&
Shiu-Ching Fan Kwok

Caroline Fei-Yeng Kwok
with her first book
The Tormented Mind

About The Author

Caroline Fei-Yeng Kwok was born in Hong Kong. After attending Ying Wa Girls' School in Hong Kong, she went to study English Literature at the University of Minnesota in 1970. She graduated with Summa Cum Laude and an Honours Award. She then returned to Hong Kong and taught English as a Second Language at the University of Hong Kong before her immigration to Canada in 1974. In 1975, Caroline received her Bachelor of Education from the University of Toronto and started teaching with the Toronto District School Board. In 1982, she received her Master of Education from the Ontario Institute For Studies In Education, University of Toronto.

In the summer of 1996, she was admitted to the Creative Writing Department at Yale University. Prior to her admission, three of her articles were published in the *Toronto Star*. In 2001, she attended the Humber School for Writers' Summer Program in Toronto. She studied at the New York State Summer Writers' Institute in 2004.

In 2001, Caroline was the recipient of the 2001 **Courage To Come Back Award** sponsored by the Centre for Addiction and Mental Health in Toronto.

Caroline is a published writer. Her articles have appeared in ***Psychiatric Services***, ***Cross Currents*** and ***Visions Magazine***. She is the author of ***The Tormented Mind***. ***Free to Fly*** is an account of her own experience as a Chinese woman afflicted with manic-depression.

FOREWORD

Caroline Fei-Yeng Kwok has had first hand experience with mental illness and has put that experience into beautiful words so that everyone can benefit. She describes her difficult times, her treatments and her mistreatments. She also describes her recovery. Seven dimensions of recovery from mental illnesses have recently been more explicitly delineated (1). The first has to do with independence in decision-making. This was difficult for Fei-Yeng to achieve because she came from a culture that valued submission and co-dependence. Obedience is what her parents expected of her and she yielded, even though she now lived in North America and autonomy is what she secretly yearned for. It led to difficulties in her relationship with her mother and meant that, despite the closeness that had always existed within her family, she had to look elsewhere to establish a network of friends who could provide support she needed – the second listed dimension of recovery. She also had to adopt a new social role once she lost her previous three identities, those of a wife, a traditional Chinese woman, a teacher. It was when she assumed her new role as writer that her recovery began. She also worked with a trusted therapist and chose to stay on medication – even though wrongful prescription of medication had almost killed her.

Emotional intelligence is another dimension of recovery. Fei-Yeng is a person who does not rein in her emotions. She expresses them to herself, to her confidants and to her readers. Healthy communication of emotion is important. Also important is that Fei-Yeng does not inhabit a world of fantasy; she lives in the world as it is and deals with all the details of everyday life–cooking, scheduling conflicting time commitments, visiting, traveling and doing her best to help others. Her work at Across Boundaries has given her life extra meaning–the knowledge that she is working within the Mental Health System, improving the quality of life for others. She has developed a strong sense of who she is, what her purpose is on earth and what the future holds. She demonstrates that recovery is there to be seized and cherished, that healing is possible even after several bouts of serious illness. Her story of self-determination will empower others and bring them comfort. She has suffered, as this book makes clear, but has transformed her suffering into hope.

Mary V. Seeman, O.C. MDCM, FRCPC
Professor Emerita
Department of Psychiatry
University of Toronto
March 23, 2006

1. Ahern L, Fisher D. Recovery at your own PACE (Personal Assistance in Community Existence). J. Psychosoc Nurs Ment Health Serv. 2001;39:22-32.

All our dreams can come true--

If we have the courage to pursue them.

--Walt Disney (1901-1966)

PREFACE

I am a Chinese woman who was formally diagnosed in 1980 in Canada as having Bipolar Affective Disorder. In layman's terms, I am a manic-depressive. In short, I am a psychiatric patient.

According to NAMI (The National Alliance for the Mentally Ill), "Manic-depression involves mood swings with some degree of depression alternating with periods of mania or elation. The cycles vary in their degree of intensity. The euphoric side of the disorder is the *mania,* while the down side is the *depression.*"

Being Chinese myself, I am well aware of the insensitivity towards and ignorance of mental illness in the Chinese community at large. However, having lived in North America for about thirty years, I am also aware that social stigma towards mental illness also exists in the so-called mainstream society. Social stigma may inhibit patients from seeking help in the initial stage of difficulty and, as a result, their illness may become more severe. To try to end social stigma is perhaps one of the major reasons for writing this book.

Through my various encounters within the mental health system, I also found that there seems to be a lack of understanding inside mental institutions with respect to patients from another culture. I hope that this book will give psychiatrists and administrators in mental institutions some insight into the problems faced by the immigrant population. Hopefully then, they will develop more cultural competence training programs.

Having been through a two-week coma as a result of neuroleptic medications, I have become very cautious of the kinds of medication, their side effects, and their high prescribed-dosages. This is especially pertinent now that recent research has demonstrated some negative long-term effects of these medications and has provided evidence for the usefulness of alternative ways of treating psychiatric illnesses. I hope that this book can help psychiatrists devise better psychiatric treatments.

Being new to Canada, I did not know the rules within mental institutions in Canada, nor was I aware of my rights as a psychiatric patient. I did not know the difference between voluntary and involuntary admissions, and was shifted from one hospital to another. Encouraging fellow sufferers to know their rights and feel empowered with the mental health system is another purpose of writing this book.

My current teaching of English as a Second Language/Literacy at *Across Boundaries* to psychiatric survivors of colour makes me realize that mental illness can affect individuals of any race, culture, or intelligence level.

Indeed, the World Health Organization (WHO) found that in 1990, unipolar major depression was the leading cause of years lived with a disability. WHO projects that by 2020, unipolar major depression will be the leading cause of disability in women and throughout the underdeveloped regions of the world. Their Globe Burden of Disease result indicates that "of the ten leading causes of disability worldwide in 1990, measured in years lived with a disability, five were psychiatric conditions: unipolar depression, alcohol use, bipolar affective disorder (manic depression), schizophrenia, and obsessive-compulsive disorder." This study also shows that "the burden of psychiatric conditions has been heavily underestimated."

The October 13, 2003 issue of *Newsweek Magazine* points out that the National Institute of Mental Health estimates that, at any age, approximately 19 million American adults suffer from a depressive disorder. The October 7, 2002 issue of the magazine reports that 3 million kids suffer from teen depression. Early untreated depression increases a youngster's chance of developing more severe depression as an adult, as well as bipolar disease and personality disorders.

An article published in October 24, 2003, *Ming Pao Daily*, a Chinese newspaper in Toronto, reported that one in five teenagers in Taiwan suffers from depression. In Hong Kong, in 2001, there were 1000 cases of suicides. There has also been a recent increase in depression among the

Hong Kong population. Ninety percent of the students in Hong Kong display symptoms of stress and anxiety.

According to the Canadian Mental Health Association's Survey, one in four Canadians suffers from mental illness. The most recent Statistics Canada Report, released at the beginning of September 2003, indicates that about 1.2 million Canadians suffer from mood disorders, including depression. Yet three out of four Canadians with a mental problem remain untreated.

It is with this new realization that I am writing this book, ***FREE TO FLY A Story of Manic Depression***.

A lot of books have been written about medical research in the field of psychiatry. But not many books have been written by women psychiatric survivors of colour such as myself. Thus, to my mind, this book could help health care professionals as well as the general public understand more about the pain that psychiatric patients go through during their time of crisis.

A final message that I hope to convey to psychiatric patients is *NOT* to give up hope. They should try their best to build up courage and act positively to fight against the social stigma of mental illness.

It is my sincere wish to let readers know that I may have an "invisible" disability, but certainly am not a waste. With determination and an inner strength, I strongly believe that we can all make our dreams become a reality.

Caroline Fei-Yeng Kwok
October, 2006

Chapter one

In The Beginning

Locked up. Locked up again—Ward 9 South of Mount Sinai Hospital here in downtown Toronto. Come to think of it, this must be my fifth time, or maybe, the tenth time. I really can't remember them all. Confused. Lost. So many hospitals. So many admissions. I am a Chinese woman afflicted with manic-depression.

Psychiatrists came to this diagnosis some twenty-five years ago. This diagnosis was beyond my comprehension. How could I, an Honours graduate from the University of Minnesota, become a psychiatric patient overnight? Could this illness be the result of my ex-husband's mental torture, the aftermath of my divorce? Or could it be that I was overworked, having to do two teaching jobs at the same time?

No. All my doctors denied such theories. It is a hereditary disease I have and for which I must take lithium for the rest of my life.

A hereditary disease? Impossible. Absolutely absurd. My parents and my aunts seem to be healthy and fit. Never have I heard of their being hospitalized in a mental institution. Could it be that my grandparents or my great-grandparents were mentally ill? Even if they were, it would have been ignored or undetected in the old days in China. Or am I the black sheep of my family? Who is to blame? God or Satan? Do I have to be locked forever in the back wards of psychiatric hospitals, having lost my mind, my dignity? Am I insane?

Then, why lithium? And for life? What are the side effects? Why not take some sleeping pills instead? Would I be able to marry again? Could I have children? Would they be deformed?

What is the definition of manic depression? I did not know much. Neither did I know its equivalence in Chinese. Based on what observations did the doctors come up with such a diagnosis? Was it my fast, accented speech that had made the doctors believe that I was having pressured speech? Or was it my aspirations that had made the doctors think that I was having grandiose thoughts? Don't forget that these are the symptoms of "manic" behavior. Or was it my distressed cries and sleepless nights over a lost love that had made the doctors think that I was depressed?

Did the doctors understand me as an individual? Or did they only see me as one of the new Asian immigrants? Did they carefully examine my chart and recognize my cultural differences? Did they know that, as a new Canadian, I was afraid of psychiatric institutions, that I did not know how to express myself to a psychiatrist during sessions, that I did not know the names of the different medications?

A hopeless nut. That was me alright. Unable to teach. Hiding behind doors. Dependent on my aging parents. Misunderstood by friends. Misjudged by relatives. Confidence lost. Self-esteem low. A living corpse with a mental handicap.

From a confident woman who went to the States to study at the age of eighteen and traveled to Europe on her own, I had become insecure, uncertain of the future. I lived in fear of having another hospitalization again.

I wanted to have friends and relatives who could understand my fears, who could give me some emotional understanding and support. But I was new to Canada then. All my long-time friends were in Hong Kong. When one was new to a country, it was difficult to find friends. I found some friends, but they were all single women who had never married. How could they understand the frustrations in my marriage? They were probably ignorant of mental illness. Unlike my long-time friends in Hong Kong, they were either in the fields of computer studies or accounting—areas that I could not relate to. They could not understand my interests in the arts either.

I sought refuge from relatives. They did not understand the nature of my illness. And many did not want to interfere with my divorce.

"It's all under the bridge now, Caroline. Don't think of your divorce

any more," they said. "Take your medications. You'll be alright."

"Just consider how lucky you are when you are in the hospital. You don't have to cook at all. And they serve you good meals every day. It's free too."

They had forgotten that what I needed most was to have an understanding and empathetic audience at the time. After all, they knew my husband too.

I tried to talk to my parents. Yet they could not understand why I had to have a divorce. They gave me lessons on the Chinese notion of loyalty and obedience.

"Why don't you listen to this old Chinese saying that once you're married, even though you have married a chicken, you should follow that chicken until you die?" My father said.

"Yes, if you had obeyed your husband and not fought with him, you would have been much happier. You wouldn't have to be sick in the hospital," echoed my mother.

They did not know of the verbal abuse and the lack of concern my husband had for me. They did not know that he just galloped his way forward without giving me a hand when I fell down from the horse. They did not know that our marriage had been incompatible and apathetic for years without much communication at all.

I did not know that there were support groups for manic-depressives. Neither did I know of courses for divorcees. Instead, I called long-distance to my girlfriends in Hong Kong, hoping that they would understand. They lent their sympathetic ears, but the calls were too costly. My telling them bits and pieces over the phone just confused them and made them more worried about me than ever.

I could not sleep very well either. Very often, I would wake up in the middle of the night, unable to go back to sleep again. This inability to sleep frustrated and agitated me. I had to take days off from my teaching job.

I listened to Chinese songs in my apartment. And I played the same

My parents and me as a bride in 1975

song over and over again:

> *"Forget about old dreams,*
> *What had gone yesterday*
> *Was dead already..."*

With a pillow over my head, I cried alone.

Who saw my silent tears, my inner fears, understood my utmost despair? Nobody. Nobody at all. *Not even God.*

I managed to smile a lot, though, in front of the others. Really smiled a lot. Should be nominated for Miss Smile of the Year. Bet I would have won. But it was just a cover-up to hide my deep melancholy, to pretend to be happy and be in tune with the world. And of course, I tried to deceive my friends and my relatives. Why should I let them know of my inner pain when they could not empathize with it? Why should I display my own fragility to them? So smile, Caroline, smile!

I was confined to the psychiatric ward of various medical institutions without choice. Involuntary admissions, that is. Not knowing much about the rules and regulations of these hospitals, I was at the mercy of the doctors and nurses. With my Chinese upbringing, I was taught to respect the doctors, the God-Almighty, without questions. Every time when I was in the hospital, I was as timid as a mouse. In short, total acceptance of the doctors' decisions and treatments.

I did not know my right as a psychiatric patient on the ward either. I was never informed of the different forms of psychiatric assessment.

What did Form I mean? I did not know that it means the person is held involuntarily for three days upon admission. To me, it only meant Grade Seven in Hong Kong. I never knew how to advocate for myself as a patient. What had happened to the courageous and articulate Caroline from Hong Kong? Were you not once the Chairperson of the Literary and Debating Club in your high school and the captain of many debates?

Being new to Canada, I did not know which hospital offers better care than the others. As a teacher, I know that the quality of schools tends to vary according to different districts. Are hospitals the same too? What is the difference between a teaching hospital and a regular hospital? Which is better?

Most of the time, I didn't dare to utter a sound in these mental institutions. Total surrender. Even more so than to Christ. In some of these institutions, if an inmate showed signs of disobedience or un-cooperation, he would probably be locked up in the quiet room. One day, one inmate, out of his own frustrations and anger, had to be locked up in a room isolated from the rest. This isolation further aggravated him. His shrieking cries for help and his banging on the wall still remain vividly in my mind. Once, I tried to be loud and rebellious. Result? Put under restraint with my hands and feet tied to the bed. Inhuman insult! Gross treatment! On another occasion, I was in a room with no bathroom. The nurse left me a bedpan next to my food tray. Loudly I cried in pain, only to find that I was put on more tranquilizers. No word of empathy. And of course, no word of comfort.

All of a sudden, I became an obedient nun in a French Abbey, counting my rosary in silence, confessing to God for my sins. Worse still, I felt as if I were a Chinese woman in World War II, being molested and raped by Japanese soldiers in the open field, receiving such torment in humiliation. Submission to force without resistance. Suppression of human rights. What agony! What cruelty!

One day, I found a piano in one of these institutions. A broken one, though. Still, it was rain after drought, sunshine after storm. I began to play my songs, songs of old and songs of new: Beethoven's Fur Elise, Bach's Minuet in G Major; John Lennon's Imagine, and Judy Collin's Both Sides Now. A group of inmates, about five or six, gathered around the piano and started singing:

> *"I've looked at life from both sides now,*
> *From win and lose, and still somehow,*
> *It's life's illusion I recall,*
> *I really don't know life at all..."*

Their voice sounded like angels from Heaven. One inmate, by the name of Melissa, started to sing *O Canada:*

> *"O Canada, our home and native land,*
> *True patriot love, in all thy sons' command,*
> *With glowing hearts, we see thee rise,*
> *The True North strong and free..."*

How patriotic! Should be the recipient of the Order of Canada. Yet never could she get this honour. A chubby nurse, the prison guard incarnate, rushed to the piano, ordered our soloist to stop and interrupted our Patients' Ensemble.

"Do you know that you're disturbing the nurses? We have to do our work in the nursing station," she said.

We looked at her in awe, afraid to talk back to her.

"Besides, music makes you too excited, hyper. Why don't you have a cup of coffee or tea in the lounge? That would calm you down."

We did not respond. Like shaggy old dogs obediently following their master, we walked behind the nurse to the lounge. There, she made her own coffee. She didn't pay any attention to us. We did not look at her either. We did not make our coffee, but only sat there silently, watching her.

Happy that we were under control, she left with her coffee. I was upset, but hid my feelings all inside. Did I dare to argue? To stand up for myself? To speak for our Patients' Ensemble? I didn't. If I did, I might be given more tranquilizers right away—uncooperative and unstable. Here in this dimly lit lounge, only one unwatered plant stood by itself. Just like the rest of the inmates, this plant was silent, voiceless.

The rest of the Ensemble did not complain, but returned, resigned, back to their own activities. James and Fred played monopoly, Gail and Gwen watched television.

Perhaps they also felt the interruption was annoying, but what could they do? Or perhaps they were immune to the authoritarianism of the mental health system and had given up their rights to speak up for themselves.

Melissa and I sat there. Composed. Quiet. Together we held our hands in alliance, blankly staring at the gray wall by the coffee corner. Spiritless. Hurt. In silence, I hummed the National Anthem of my adopted land, *O Canada.* Melissa looked at me and patted my shoulder. We understood. A battle won in desperation, in total submission.

"In the beginning
God created the Heaven and the Earth
...And God said,
'Let there be light'
and there was light..."
Genesis 1: 1-3

These are the words of God. But could we, *Patients of Psychiatric Wards,* be able to inhabit the Heaven and the Earth? Would we ever be able to hear the voices of our beloved friends and relatives? Are we allowed to love and be loved? And would we be accepted and understood?

Dear God, would you grant us,
Patients of Psychiatric Wards,
Your Light please?

Chapter Two

A LIGHT OF HOPE

From my bedroom window, I looked at the street below. Wet. Completely wet. Rain must have come a moment ago. Water from the lamppost came dripping to the sidewalk. Silent and stoic, the lamplight beamed at this forsaken street, shining like the eternal torch of the Olympics. Shed a bit of hope, perhaps, to this desolate neighborhood of mine.

Every night for the past two weeks, I had been watching this empty street and its lamplight. Tried to look for a star to comfort my anguish, a star to lift up my despair. Yet what did I see? Only darkness, with a faint light.

Tonight, just like previous nights, I could not sleep. Kept staring at the ceiling. Restless. Agitated. I got out of my bed and called long distance to my friend, Chee Man, in Hong Kong, but the phone just continued to ring. No answer. I went to the kitchen and drank a big glass of chocolate milk. Any effect? Did I become tired? Did I fall asleep? No. Not at all. I then took an hour-long foam bath. Closed my eyes and tried to relax. Any use? No. Still wide-awake.

Had I, all at once, become Shakespeare's Macbeth, crying in desperation, "Shall sleep no more! Macbeth shall sleep no more!" A law-abiding citizen always, how could I have committed a murderous crime as Macbeth and be tortured by sleepless nights? Could this ordeal be God's punishment? Or did I have to bear the sins of my parents and my ancestors? Be my family's scapegoat?

I heard the songs of the thrush from afar. I could also hear the chickadee humming his lullaby. In the distance, I saw a glimpse of sunrise. Must be dawn by now. Well, another sleepless night. Didn't really matter. I had gotten used to these torments of the mind.

I called Phillip. The telephone just kept ringing.

Who was Phillip? He was a professor in the East Asian Studies at the University of Toronto whom I met about two years ago in a Tai Chi class at the Hart House. He was a Greek-Canadian, three years older than me, born in Montreal, but studied Chinese Mythology when he had his PhD degree at the University of British Columbia. Fascinated by the Orient, he had been to South East Asia many times. We had been going out with each other since then. He was a bit taller than me, had curly dark-brown hair, and muscular in his arms. Except for his occasional cowardice, he was gentle, humorous, and kind. His parents lived in Vancouver and he was their only son.

We called each other every night, talking until the wee hours. Sometimes, he came over to my place and stayed overnight. But lately, he seemed moody. He had not been coming as often as before. Our phone conversations had become short.

"What happened? Are you mad at me?" I asked.

"No."

"Why is it that you don't seem to be with me these days?"

"Don't ask, OK? I'm fine," he snapped at me. This was not his usual behaviour. He seldom would lose his temper with me. I just assumed that it was pressure from his teaching and research.

Two weeks ago, I received a letter from him. He wrote:

Dear Caroline:

You're going to hate me when you get this letter, but I must tell you the truth. I cannot see you anymore for the reason that I will have to marry Anastasia, my former Greek girlfriend, in about a month from now. My parents are very conservative and want me to marry a Greek woman. See, I am their only son. I feel that I am obligated to fulfill their wish. After all, they immigrated to Canada pinning all their hopes on me. I can't disappoint them.

I love you very much, my dear Caroline. But what can I do? Sometimes, we have to submit ourselves to the reality of life. Love and marriage are two different things.

In fact, it had taken days for me to write this letter. Perhaps now, you understand why I was so snappy for the past weeks or so. I was angry at myself and I had a hard time deciding too. I know that this will hurt you. It tortures my heart to see you cry. That's why I am sending this letter to you instead of telling you in person.

Past is past. We did have a good time together, didn't we? For that, I will always treasure you in my heart. I will always remember the wooden China Doll that you gave me for my birthday present a year ago. I hope that you will also keep my Venus Goddess of Love necklace.

Love,
Phillip

I could not believe my eyes when I read the letter. Just a week earlier, he was in my apartment. He told me that he loved me very much. How could he just discontinue our relationship with only a letter, without saying any words of good-bye in person? How could he be so cruel to me whom he made love to so passionately just a few days ago?

I called Phillip again. There was no answer except for the same old voice mail, "this is 416-972-8163. No one is available at the moment. Please leave a message and I will return your call as soon as possible." Where was he? Did he deliberately want to ignore my calls? Did he really mean to say good-bye forever? Yet did he not answer every one of my calls just two months ago?

More frustrated than ever, I went to the kitchen to have my breakfast. Yet I wasn't hungry at all. Just kept looking at the bowl of cereal. Come to think of it, I hadn't been eating for the past two days. Yet surprisingly, I did not feel hungry. I then went to the bathroom and tried to get ready to go to work. How appalling it was to see myself in the mirror! A vampire from the underworld, a mummy from an Egyptian tomb. Dark eyebags, greasy hair, swollen face. Only last month I was a young woman with a photogenic face and an enticing smile, full of charm and

spirit. What had I become in an instant? A wrinkled bag lady, a battered whore—tired and exhausted, dirty and smelly. That was me alright. Yet as obstinate as ever, I still insisted on going to teach. A dedicated hero. A devoted teacher. How lofty! How admirable!

"Are *you* Ms. Kwok? I can't believe it! *You* really look beat! What happened to your hair? Did you put gel in? It looks so greasy! And your face looks so pale. Are you alright?" All of my students were stunned.

"I'm fine, really. Just didn't sleep very well for a few days. I can manage. Don't worry, class."

I tried to talk in my usual calm manner. But behind this calmness were fears, anguish, and feelings of intimidation, something that I had not experienced in the past.

Obediently the students opened their books. I started reading Chapter One of Charles Dickens' *A Tale of Two Cities.*

> *"It was the best of time, it was the worst of times, it was the age of wisdom, it was the age of foolishness, it was the epoch of belief, it was the epoch of incredulity, it was the season of light, it was the season of darkness, it was the Spring of hope, it was the Winter of despair..."*

But I couldn't concentrate, neither could I comprehend. Muttered inconsistent words, mumbled irrelevant ideas. My hands shook and my body shivered. I simply couldn't continue with the lesson.

The students stared at me in awe, shocked. There was not a sound in the classroom. At lunchtime, the principal came to my workroom. He was in his late-fifties and came from Trinidad and Tobago.

"Caroline, I can see that you don't feel well."

"How do you know?" Instantly I responded, suspicious of his remark, afraid that the students had reported my behaviour to him.

"I just sort of noticed. Don't be uptight. How have you been lately? Have you been eating well? You look devastated today."

"Well, to tell you the truth, Mr. Dick, I've not been sleeping at all for the past few days. Really, every night is an agony. And I'm all by myself."

"Yes, I remember you told me that your mother does not live with you anymore. Where does she live now?"

"She has been living in Supportive Housing on Yonge and Eglinton since 1992."

"And your dad passed away in the eighties, if I remember well."

"Yes, in 1984."

"Does your mother know that you have sleeping problems?"

"Of course not. Please don't tell her. She'll force me to take medicine as she did in Hong Kong."

"Don't worry, I won't. But, Caroline, it's important that you see a doctor. I mean, a psychiatrist."

"A psychiatrist? My! My Chinese friends will ostracize me. They'll call me Ms. Crazy or Ms. Fruitcake. I don't want to be sent to those mental hospitals in Hong Kong."

"Hold it, Caroline. Calm down. Don't panic. This is Canada, *not* Hong Kong. Besides, you *won't* lose your job with our school board. Go to the Ontario Secondary School Teachers' Federation and apply for a disability pension. Once the school board doctor says that you are fit to return to school, you will. You're always a good teacher and many students like you. Believe me, I wouldn't like to lose such an excellent teacher like you. Just see the doctor, take the medications, and rest. I'm sure that you'll be able to return to work soon. Trust me, I'm the principal."

"You're sure?" I asked, still uncertain. Teaching is extremely important to me. After all, had I not spent years getting my credentials in Canada? I could not afford to stay at home. I would die from boredom. Besides, my mother, who did not understand the school system, would keep nagging me.

"One-hundred percent positive, my dear Ms. Kwok. You'll be reinstated back to work once you get a clean bill of health."

"OK, Mr. Dick. I'll listen to you then. I never knew that you're so understanding. I always thought that principals are cold and uncaring."

Mr. Dick smiled. "Oh, call me once you're home. Just to make sure that you're safe and sound."

I didn't go home right away. Why should I? What was there at home? Nothing—no foods, no visitors, and no Phillip. Worse than the isolated towns in California. Why should I be like Shirley Valentine, talking alone in the kitchen to the blank wall? And should I be Katherine Hepburn delivering Cleopatra's soliloquy in an empty theatre?

I decided to wander along Danforth Avenue. The sky and the clouds were much better to look at. There on Danforth Avenue were many little Greek restaurants.

It was in the Friendly Greek Restaurant where Phillip and I had our first date. That was one evening in May, 1995. The weather was more or less the same as it was today. We ordered a Greek salad, a Souvlakia for me, a Vegetarian Moussaka for him, and two Baklavas for dessert. And of course, a bottle of red wine.

"Are you a vegetarian?" I asked.

"Yes, I am," he said. He gave me an intriguing look with his brownish eyes. "Just like a Buddhist monk."

I was amused and surprised. Over dinner, he told me of his interests in Chinese Mythology. He also told me stories of Greek gods—Apollo, Aphrodite, Dionysus, and the rest. He told me the tale of Hero and Leander, of how they lived on opposite banks of the Hellespont, of how the two lovers had met at the Festival of Adonis, and of how Leander vowed to swim across the river to see Hero every night to prove his love to her.

"What happened?" I said, fascinated.

"Well, one night during a storm, Hero's lamp blew out and Leander lost his way. The next morning, Hero looked out to see his body lying on

the rocks at the foot of her tower. She was so distressed she threw herself down to join him in death."

I was moved. He looked at me and said, "I'll be Hero to you too."

How sweet! To be willing to die for me! I was impressed.

Yet now, it was also May. What had happened to him? He had deserted me for another woman. I felt that I was a fool, too naïve to have believed in his sweet talks. I could not understand his cowardice either. To submit to the wish of his parents in his decision to marry? How could a well-educated man be so obedient to his parents? Was it true or just a lie? An excuse to end his relationship with me?

I could feel the spring breeze around me. Summer would be here soon. Wouldn't it be nice to go to Center Island for a picnic then and go for the rides in its amusement park?

I walked along Bloor Street. Its big department stores attracted me. It would be nice to buy a pair of sandals or a nice blouse from Holt Renfrew for the summer, wouldn't it? Yet I only had twenty dollars. I continued to walk until I reached Spadina Avenue and Dundas Street near Chinatown. The restaurants and shops had neon lights with big Chinese characters. Chinese music could be heard on the streets. And hawkers were selling vegetables and fruits on Dundas Street too.

The streetcars were running with cars jammed on the roads. Yes, Chinatown, one of the favorite places that Phillip and I liked to go. I remembered how we held hands during the Chinese New Year's Bazaar and all the lovely Chinese dishes that we had. Did he not tell me that he loved me in one of these restaurants? Where was he now? I walked among the crowd, hoping to find Phillip. But no Phillip.

Dr. Joseph Wong's office was close to Chinatown. Yet somehow, I was apprehensive. Dr. Wong had been my family physician since 1991. Six years now. He was about my age and a caring doctor who knew me well. He wouldn't execute me as those Japanese soldiers did to the Chinese during the Massacre of Nanking. Doctors are to heal, not to kill. But

why, all at once, this fear? Should I see him? Or should I go home?

Like a ship captain lost in the Bermuda Triangle, I walked around the blocks in Chinatown in a circle. Suddenly, I saw my lighthouse—the telephone booth. I took out a quarter and dialed. Yes, I should call Joe. No. He had a board meeting today. Or maybe, I'd call Shirley. But she would be busy babysitting. Should I call my mother? Yes, why not? But she would rush me to the hospital as she did in Hong Kong. Besides, she's too old and doesn't speak English anyway. A long-distance call to Chee Man in Hong Kong would be the best. She would understand. We've been good pals since high school. But did I have enough money to make the call? Besides, it was their midnight. I put my quarter back into my purse. Just like a lone pilgrim looking for the Holy Grail, I continued my journey, in search of an answer and a destination.

I became the twentieth century Hamlet, "To be or not to be, that is the question." I also became the personification of T. S. Eliot's Prufrock, "in a minute, there is time. For decisions and revisions which a minute will reverse." Decisions, hesitations, indecisions.

After much debate, I walked into Dr. Wong's office. The waiting room was quite small, but was nicely carpeted with Chinese paintings on the wall. Karen, his secretary, was busy on the phone. There were quite a few patients ahead of me. I became agitated and started pacing restlessly back and forth in the room.

"Caroline, come on in," said Dr. Wong as he opened his office door. "You don't look like your usual self. Why? You seem exhausted and hyper. What's wrong? Tell me."

I couldn't control my tears.

"Well, to be honest with you, Dr. Wong, I haven't been sleeping for the past few days. And I haven't been eating well either. By the way, can I have a glass of water? I've been walking all over town for two or three hours."

"Sure, why not?" Dr. Wong handed me a paper cup with icy cold

water. "You mean, in this heat? Caroline, why didn't you come to see me earlier? What's bothering you? You don't have to be afraid. I'm your doctor."

"I know, Dr. Wong. But it's quite embarrassing to talk to you about it. Remember our mutual friend, Phillip? The Greek-Canadian professor in East Asian Studies at the University of Toronto? Well, he and I were with each other for the past two years or so. We talked practically every night, even when he was at conferences in Hawaii and Singapore. And of course, we made love. It was just wonderful. We were just like newlyweds and I thought that this was love. I was wrong." More tears rolled down my face. Dr. Wong handed me a tissue.

"Continue, Caroline. You're doing fine."

"See, about two weeks ago, Phillip sent me a letter and told me that he can't see me anymore. He told me that his former girlfriend, Anastasia, is back in his life. His family in Vancouver pressures him to marry her. All of a sudden, he cut me off. Remember the book that you told me about? *I Never Promised You A Rose Garden.* Life is *not* a rose garden, neither is love. I know that. And I'm not Cinderella either," I said as I wiped my tears.

"I understand, Caroline. We're only human beings with all our frailties."

"You're right, Dr. Wong. But what I detest most is that Phillip *lied behind my back!* How come he wasn't honest with me in the first place? Why did he say that he loves me? *A pack of lies!*"

"Maybe he is a coward after all and doesn't want to face direct confrontations with you. Do you know that very often, men are more cowardly than women? Did you tell your friends about your problem?"

"You want me to get killed, Dr. Wong? Most of my friends here are very Chinese. Or, should I say, puritanical and moralistic. They are mainly single women who have never married. Would they be able to understand? If they knew that I had an affair with a non-Chinese man, they would probably think that I was a whore. Don't forget, Dr. Wong,

I was divorced some fifteen years ago. In those days, I hardly had any friends at all. Why don't you give me some Ativan? It always works. I'll be alright."

"Caroline, your problem is more than just insomnia. I can't prescribe sleeping pills to you this time."

"Why?"

"You have to see a psychiatrist."

"A psychiatrist? My principal told me the same thing this morning. Hey, would I be put in a straightjacket? Do I have to go through electric shock treatment?"

"I don't think so, Caroline. In fact, straightjackets don't exist in Canada anymore. So, don't be afraid. Just wait outside for a moment. After I call Mount Sinai Hospital, I'll drive you there."

Afraid of the unknown, worried about the diagnosis and exhausted from sleepless nights, I couldn't help crying out loud. I was like a young mother mourning over the death of her child killed in a bombshell in Ho Chi Minh City during the Vietnam War.

Dr. Wong was shocked. Never had he seen me in this desolate state.

"Don't cry, Caroline. You'll be OK. Be brave. Remember Napoleon Bonaparte, the hero that you often told me about? He fought, he lost, and he still fought until the end. You can do that too, can't you? I promise I'll visit you."

I waited for Dr. Wong in the waiting room. As I looked at the Chinese paintings on the wall, my Chinese philosophy came back. All at once, I remembered the saying of dissolving one's sorrow and anger into strength that my mother taught me when I was little. Yes, I should learn to be strong when faced with adversities. Why should I let Phillip bother me?

After a while, Dr. Wong came out of his office. He turned off the lights before we left the office. The office was as dark as a jungle. So was University Avenue. Had I lost my direction again in a moonless night, this time in the South China Sea?

Stars, bright stars, where are you? Are you also lost in the dark? Give me some lights! Yes, lights to light up the candle of my heart, my candle of hope and courage. Wind, I can hear your ferocious voice. But, dear gentle wind, please don't blow my candle out!

Dear God,
Show me Your Stars,
And Your Lights,
Please.

Chapter three

Songs Of Comfort

Motionless, I sat in Dr. Wong's car, afraid to speak a word. Quiet as a church mouse I was. Dr. Wong was silent.

The silence appalled me. I looked out the window of his 1986 Volvo, trying to look for a star—a star that would brighten my moment of darkness, my anguish. Silently, I hoped to see a star that would make me forget Phillip. Yet I could not find one.

Had I, because of my illness, suddenly become Laura in the Glass Menagerie? Or had I become a crippled tree? God, listen to my prayer, would you? Help my mother and my close friends understand about my illness, that a "disabled" person like myself can love and be loved, can help and be helped. God, help them to understand that I'm not Van Gogh's sunflower, but a shining star. Dear God, who am I? A puppet on the stage? An actor for people to criticize? No dignity? No emotions? A crazy fool?

I looked at the ebony sky again. No stars. A dream, perhaps.

Eventually, Dr. Wong broke the silence.

"Caroline, how come you're so quiet?"

"I'm a bit scared."

"Don't worry. Just be calm. We're about to arrive at the hospital."

"OK. I'll try."

Dr. Wong parked his car at the emergency entrance. There were some ambulances there. In the emergency room, nurses and doctors ran back and forth with charts and syringes, as if they were self-proclaimed guardian angels of the lost moaning souls.

The registration clerk called my name from the counter. "What's your OHIP number?"

"Do you have a Mount Sinai Hospital Card?"

"Can you fill out the form please? Write down your address and phone number."

Like a student writing for the examination, I carefully wrote the information down.

"Who should we contact in case of emergency?"

I looked at Dr. Wong. Should I write down my mother's name? But she did not speak English. What's the use?

"Can I use your name instead, Dr. Wong?"

"OK. That's fine." He probably understood the language barrier of a Chinese senior like my mother.

"Why don't you wait in the examination room down by the hall?" Said the clerk.

Both Dr. Wong and I went into the room. It was dismal and plain. No paintings. No coffee pots. Only two wooden chairs. Outside, there was a desk for the nurses. On the desk were syringes, cotton balls, tongue depressors, and stethoscopes. In another room lay an old man moaning about his stomach pain.

We waited for a long time. I was thirsty and hungry.

"Nurse, can I have a glass of water please?" I asked.

"No, you can't until you've been seen by the doctor," answered the nurse in her professional manner. She went back to do her charts.

Silence. Pure silence. This silence suffocated my mind. I couldn't stand it anymore. I quietly sang my favorite song, *We Shall Overcome*:

"We shall overcome
We shall overcome
We shall overcome some day,
Oh, deep in my heart,
I do believe that
We shall overcome some day."

To my surprise, Dr. Wong joined in. All at once, we became a duet on the stage. Together both doctor and patient joined in the fight against the battle of mental illness.

"We are not afraid
We are not afraid
We are not afraid today,
Oh deep in my heart,
I do believe that
We shall overcome some day."

A young, blonde lady came to the room. She had a note pad.

"My name is Rosa and I am the social worker. Caroline, can you tell me a bit about your family? Who lives with you? Where do you work? What do you do? What medications are you taking?"

Why did she want to know? Would she be able to help me? Nervously I looked at Dr. Wong for assurance.

"Go on, Caroline. Tell Rosa everything," said Dr. Wong.

Hesitantly, I told her that I had been in Canada since 1974, divorced, and had been living alone since. I told her that I am a teacher, teaching English as a Second Language with the Toronto District School Board. I also told her that my mother, who used to live in the same apartment building, had been living in Supportive Housing since 1992.

"Why?" Rosa asked.

"You have to ask Dr. Wong," I said.

"I'll tell you later," said Dr. Wong.

"What brings you here today?"

"Well, I haven't been sleeping for the past few days and haven't been eating well. When I was at school this morning, I could not concentrate. The principal told me to see a doctor."

"Why is it that you couldn't sleep?"

At that moment, I could not control my emotions. Tears came onto my face. My hands shook. I paused for a moment.

"'Cause my boyfriend, Phillip, deserted me!"

"It's OK, Caroline. It's not the end of the world," consoled Rosa. She kindly gave me a tissue to wipe my tears. "Just calm down. The doctor will be here in a minute."

She jotted down the information in her note pad. Then, she left.

We waited for another half an hour before a male doctor came in. He was a Caucasian, about thirty years old, neatly dressed with a tie, tall and skinny, and wore a pair of brown glasses.

"I'm Dr. James. You must be Caroline, and you, Dr. Wong. How are you, Caroline?"

"Fine," timidly I answered.

Dr. James looked at me. He was, to me, the untouchable God of my fate.

"Dr. Wong, can I talk to you outside for a minute?"

"Sure, no problem."

Dr. Wong left with Dr. James to the other room.

I was left in the room all by myself. Sweat, tears, and fears. What would happen to me? What would my future be? My sanity nearly lost in this silence. To comfort myself, I began to sing again. This time, it was my favorite song from *Les Miserables:*

> *"Do you hear the people sing,*
> *Singing the songs of angry men.*
> *This is the music of a people,*
> *Who will not be slaves again.*
> *When the beating of the heart,*
> *Echoes the beating of the drums,*
> *There is a life about to start,*
> *When tomorrow comes."*

Dr. James and Dr. Wong came back into the room.

"Caroline, you sing too loud. Keep your voice down," Dr. James said.

"Why can't I sing?" I protested.

"Well, you're disturbing other patients. This is a hospital, not a theatre. Also, you're too hyper. Caroline, calm down. Let me ask you a few questions."

"Dr. James, can I have some water please? I'm extremely thirsty."

"OK," he left the room and came back with a glass of water.

Slowly I drank the water.

"Could I have something to eat? I'm hungry too."

"Well, I'm afraid that you'll have to wait until afterwards."

Who could understand my inner pain? My inner fears? No, nobody. Suddenly, I became one of the three blind mice, at the mercy of this tall doctor, Dr. James. Dr. Wong looked on.

"Now, answer these questions for me, Caroline. Do you know what day is it today?"

"What year and what month?"

"Where are you now?"

"What city are you in now?"

"Can you repeat 'no, its, ands, and buts' after me?"

"Repeat the words, chair, wall, and floor, to me."

"Subtract seven from one hundred and keep going."

"Spell the word 'world' backward."

"Can you remember those three words again?"

Nervously I answered the questions. I knew that I was rambling at the same time. But it was my usual self when I was in panic. Did I give the correct answers? Could he clearly understand my replies in my accented English? What if I didn't know English?

The ordeal of this test reminded me of the English oral examination that I had to go through for the High School Public Examination in Hong Kong. More anxious than ever, I began to cry again.

"That's OK, Caroline. Now can you pick up the paper that is on the floor?" said Dr. James as he dropped the paper on the floor. "Fold the paper, and give it to me. That's it."

He then gave me another piece of paper. "Now, draw a clock and put the hand at ten after eleven."

I could not draw. I failed drawing in high school. Still, I tried my best.

"Can you write a sentence for me? Can you write 'I am in Mount Sinai Hospital now'?"

I looked at Dr. James again. Why did I have to write a sentence? But I did not dare to ask.

"Now obey me when I say 'close your eyes'"

I started singing the tune that I made for Phillip: "Close your eyes, you're tired tonight, forget, forget, forget your woes…"

"No, Caroline. I don't want you to sing. I want you to obey me when I say 'close your eyes'."

Confused. These questions didn't mean anything to me. Never had I to answer these questions when I sat in for my University Entrance Examination. Am I a "retard"? Why these questions? To test my IQ?

Dr. James looked at his notes.

"I think that you should stay as an in-patient in the psychiatric ward for a period of time."

"No Way! I won't! You've no right to lock me up!" Loudly I yelled. More tears rolled down my swollen face.

That was my primal response. And, of course, it made Dr. James feel that I was sicker than ever.

"Well, Caroline, you suffer from bipolar affective disorder."

"What?"

"In other words, manic-depression. It means that you have mood swing, ranging from being depressed to manic."

Shivering and shaking, I cried. I didn't want to be locked up. What did he mean by depressed? And manic? What were the symptoms? I did not know. He never told me.

All I wanted was some understanding and comfort to help me overcome my crisis with Phillip. How could Dr. James be able to diagnose me within half an hour? And he never asked me any questions as to what triggered my behavior.

Dr. Wong was there. What could he have done? He was only a family physician and not a psychiatrist in the hospital. He could only give suggestions about treatments.

"Dr. Wong, what should I do?"

"Don't worry, Caroline. Just listen to what Dr. James told you. Remember the song that we sang, *We Shall Overcome?* You shouldn't be afraid and you *will* overcome. Just take it easy and relax. I believe in you."

Dr. Wong gave me an encouraging smile and patted my shoulder. Doubtfully, I looked at him. I became calmer.

"Can you go up to the ward with me?"

"No, I can't, Caroline. Don't worry. I'll visit you for sure and I'll call your mother for you. I promise. Don't cry and be strong. Remember, I'm your doctor and also your friend."

Yes, I should be strong. Didn't my mother always teach me to be strong? She had a tough life, having to go through the Second World War and the Japanese Occupation in China. Yet she survived, right? And I must consider myself lucky to be able to speak English to answer those questions. What about those immigrants who can't speak the language? They would have been more intimidated by the doctors and the hospital than me.

All at once, I remembered what my father told me once, "Courage, my dear daughter." Yes, with courage, I would seek help in the psychiatric ward of Mount Sinai Hospital. Why should I be afraid?

I wiped my tears. Dr. Wong left and I was alone with Dr. James. He gave me a syringe. Up I went with him and the paramedics to the ninth floor of the hospital to Ward 9 South, the psychiatric ward for in-patients. That was it, no exit. Another involuntary admission. Another solitary confinement. Oh God, when would I be able to get out? And when would I see my star in the sky again?

For the moment, I was only a Chinese golden bird locked in an iron cage, singing silently, slowly weeping, *We Shall Overcome.*

Dear God,
Give me Your Courage,
Please.

Chapter four

NO EXIT

Right after the paramedics had left me in the ward, the door slammed behind me. I tried to open this Gate of Hell. Only then did I realize that I was being held by two security guards. Locked again. Another imprisonment. No exit. Yes, no exit for sure.

To the left of the hall was the nursing station with glass windows. A receptionist was at the front, busy working with her chart. To the right were the patients' rooms. Further down was the common lounge. Right at the end of the hall was a baby grand piano with dining tables next to it. Around the corner were more patients' rooms and a smoking room. One patient with a bloated face sat on one of the chairs in the hall, his hands trembling. Another sat motionless, staring into the distance as if he were in a trance.

A nurse in her mid-thirties with short, brownish hair came to greet me.

"My name is Marilyn. I will be your primary nurse. Come, take off your clothes, take a shower perhaps, and then, change into the hospital gown," said the nurse as she showed me to my room. She also handed me the blue hospital gown.

"I'll take your clothes and your purse after you have changed."

"What?"

"Just to store them in the safe so that nobody will take them. I'll be back in a second."

After she left, I was alone in the room. I began my journey of exploration. The room itself was America and I was Christopher Columbus. A spacious room it was with a shower, four single beds with clean bed sheets, and four end tables. There were no pictures on the wall. The wide window overlooked University Avenue, the Toronto General Hospital and the Hospital for Sick Children. Shall I call this temporary shelter of mine Park Hyatt Hotel or Four Seasons' Sheraton?

Nurse Marilyn came back with the medications and the blood pressure monitor. I had already taken a shower and changed to the hospital gown.

"Your blood pressure is perfect—125 over 82. Now, take the medications."

"What are they?" I asked.

"They are clonazapam, epival, lithium, and haloperidol."

Worried about their side effects, but afraid to ask, I was hesitant to take them.

"Don't worry, Caroline. You have to listen to me. Just take the medications and get well. You see, this is not an asylum, as you may think. It's a place for you to rest and you'll get out when you feel better. Just try to cooperate, OK?"

She held my arms with such warmth and sounded as if she were the Archangel from Heaven. Could it be that she was really concerned about me? Or was it only part of her professional etiquette?

Like an obedient child, I closed my eyes and swallowed them at once.

I was just wondering who my roommate would be when, all of a sudden, a Chinese woman walked into the room. She was in her late twenties with heavy make-up on her oval face. Her brownish-black hair was short.

"Hey, you must be a new arrival, right?"

"Yes. Just came a few minutes ago."

"My name is Jen and I'm from Taiwan. I bet you're Chinese too, right?"

"Yes, I am from Hong Kong, but have lived in Canada for over twenty years now."

"Wow! I have only lived in Canada for about seven years. You mean there *are* crazy Chinese like you and me?"

Loud giggles.

"Jen, how long have you been in this nuthouse?"

"You mean this Torture Chamber?"

"Yes, of course." Another laugh.

"Well, for about three months now. On and off. Schizophrenic."

"Oh, I'm a manic-depressive."

"I guess that both of us are nuts, eh?"

"Hazelnut or walnut?"

A roar of laughter again.

Delighted and excited, I laughed heartily for the first time in a month. A big release of suppressed emotions. Even a mental derelict like myself needs a spark of life once in a while. But, Caroline, watch out. This sudden burst of laughter is a sign of uncontrolled, inappropriate behavior. Unstable, the doctors say. So, better be calm, sit properly, read a Chinese magazine, talk quietly to your visitors, and remember to always close the door. Be a perfect little China Doll.

Why should I complain? Why should I be unhappy? I had found an oasis in the middle of the Sahara Desert, a lighthouse in the midst of a rough sea.

Meals were served in the lunchroom every day at approximately the same time: juice and cereal for breakfast, salad and soup for lunch, meat and pasta for dinner. How delicious! And of course, there was plenty of milk, juice, and yogurt in the refrigerator in the common lounge too. Most of the time, like the nuns in the nunnery, meals were eaten in silence. Probably, we, the inmates of the ward, were either too drowsed off with the medications, or so absorbed with our own problems. After meals, some would resign back to their rooms while others would gather in the only social gathering area--the smoking room. Behind its closed door, confessions were made among ourselves, without the presence of the Holy Father, of course.

Every morning, at around seven-thirty, Ruth, Mother Superior of my

Holy Refuge, would give me medications, about five or six pills of various colours. United Nations, that was what I called them. Didn't know much about their side effects, still I swallowed them without any questions, pretending that they were my favorite candies. Did I dare to argue? Did I dare to refuse? No. Got no guts. Didn't want to be a permanent resident in this first-class hotel. Remember Nurse Marilyn? No medications, no exit. So smarten up, Caroline! Take all the damn pills!

Once, in the early days of my admission, I refused to take the medication.

"What is this pill?" Defiantly I asked.

"It's haloperidol," said Nurse Winnie.

"*I won't take it. Dr. Lemke says that I'm not psychotic!*" I yelled. Dr. Lemke, a young resident, was one of my favorite psychiatrists whom I had seen before my admission. Haloperidol is a major anti-psychotic neuroleptic medication.

"Dr. Lemke is not your psychiatrist in this ward now. The doctor here thinks that you should take it. It's the doctor's order, I'm afraid. Come on, be nice."

Out of fear perhaps, I just ran all the way to the end of the hall, only to be caught by another nurse. And of course, my behaviour would make these nurses think that I was more manic than ever.

The nurses would talk to me every day. Nurse Marilyn, Nurse Natalie, and Nurse Pat. They were extremely patient and kind. Yet not knowing of the importance of talk therapy, I hid my feelings all inside. I just answered their questions in the most cooperative manner as I could. Afraid that I might have to remain in the hospital, I did not expose my true emotions. Why should I tell them about Phillip and me? Would they be able to help me? Would they be able to understand my feelings as a Chinese woman born in Hong Kong, educated in the States, who had lived in Canada for over twenty-five years? They had never lived or traveled to Hong Kong. Besides, they were not my girlfriends from Hong

Kong who had known me well from elementary school.

Instead, I wrote my feelings down in Chinese. I started to write poems. Even though I showed some of my poems to these nurses, they could not understand. And my translation wasn't very good either. This left me more frustrated than ever.

Dr. Wendy Yiu was assigned to me as my in-patient psychiatrist. In her early thirties, she too was Chinese-Canadian, but could only speak "broken Cantonese" with a heavy accent and could not read or write Chinese. Unlike me, she came with her parents to Alberta at the age of four. She wore a pair of black-framed glasses, had straight short hair, "slanted" eyes, and always liked to wear her long dress as if she were going to a ball. I didn't like her at all at first glance. Her look reminded me so much of my ex-husband. There was little empathy between she and me. Yet, in the eyes of the other doctors, they probably would think that we had a good therapeutic alliance for the reason that we were both Chinese.

For the few weeks after the haloperidol incident, Dr. Yiu isolated me to a single room with a private bath, two nursing assistants, Maria and Ellen, and a security guard, George, barring the entrance of my room. Why she had given me this "royal first class treatment" in this Mount Sinai Hotel, I did not know. Perhaps she thought that I was uncooperative and would run away?

Maria was an immigrant from Trinidad and Tobago. Short and chubby and in her early forties, she always greeted me with a smile. She and I shared a lot of jokes. We also shared our common experience as immigrants.

"It's nice that you are a teacher. Me, I was a nurse in my own country, but now, I can only work as a nursing assistant."

"Why?" I asked.

"Because in Canada, I have to have Canadian experience and qualifications in order to be a nurse. I can't afford the time to study because I have three kids at home to look after."

She also brought me back to Christ. We sang hymns together: *Onward Christian Soldiers, Joy Is Like The Rain,* and *Thank You.* Singing hymns in this moment of distress was a great comfort for me. All of a sudden, I was in my high school, singing hymns for our daily morning assemblies. She also "invented" the old Chinese way of blood circulation exercises. And she even smuggled some delicious Caribbean food to me.

Ellen, in her late twenties, was from the Philippines and was equally patient with me. She was in distress herself. Her husband had lost his job and she found out that she was pregnant. She had to give me a bath every day. I had to undress right in front of her. What a disgrace! Had I suddenly become incapable of taking care of myself?

George, the security guard, was very strict with me. If I simply peeped through my door, he would reproach me. He did not understand my frustrations, my loneliness, and my fears, having to be kept in a room, not knowing about the exact date of my release.

"You've got to stay in your room. If you cross the line, I'll have to ask the nurse to give you medications."

What had I done wrong? Had I committed a serious offence and had to be detained in an isolation cell, as if I were a young offender, waiting for my trial at the Toronto Youth Assessment Center? Or had I, all at once, become a black slave in America in the olden days, having to be segregated from the whites?

I did not dare to express my feelings to this guard. Yet at the bottom of my heart, I wondered who had given him the permission to threaten me. A patient such as myself who, at that time, needed care and comfort, was most fragile. An intimidation such as this would only worsen my state of mind. A prisoner I was, kept behind bars without any hope for parole. I had not committed a crime. Why should I deserve these verbal assaults?

When could I be free and be able to reach out to the sky, to see the seagulls flying by? When would I see God's Light and His mercy?

"Why can't I cross the line?" I said.

"Caroline, this is the doctor's order. You had better listen. If you don't, I will report it to the nurses. They may put you in restraint."

Immediately, I became a timid mouse, kept in a cage for my master to look at. Freedom lost. No talking back. Hurrah! Master, you won! You are the God-Almighty Lion and I am a poor little obedient mouse. So, Caroline, shut up! Don't ever give him the excuse to put you in restraint. The more cooperative you are, the faster you can get out of the ward. Forget what you have read in the books about the theories of psychiatric treatments.

I regained my temporary freedom from George after a few weeks. I was allowed to go back to the room with my roommates.

"Welcome back, Caroline," said Jen.

"How have you been?"

"Well, the same. Still on risperidone, chlorpromazine, and olanzapine."

"Tell me, Jen. How come you have to be in the hospital in the first place?"

"To tell you the truth, this is my second hospitalization. When I first came to Toronto seven years ago, I was studying at George Brown College, taking my computer courses. But I found that I could not concentrate on my study and showed no interest in my study at all. Probably it had to do with my new adjustment to Canada and my English wasn't very good then. I dropped out of college. Don't forget that when I was in Taiwan, I topped my class. Then, I became socially withdrawn from my friends and was not interested in any activities at all. I began to hear voices telling me to kill myself."

"Did you?"

"No, I didn't. If I did, I wouldn't be here today," Jen laughed. "My parents noticed the change in me and they took me to the doctor who diagnosed me as a schizophrenic. See, my parents still don't understand why I dropped out of George Brown. They are disappointed in me. After all, they gave up everything in Taiwan to come to Toronto, hoping to have a better life for me."

"Well, don't feel guilty about it. It's your health that matters, right?"

"It's nice that I ran into you, Caroline. You and I are both Chinese and are in the same boat. At least you understand me and we can support each other. See, a lot of Chinese despise mental illness."

"Yes, I know. It's a shame."

"We will keep in touch with each other once we are out, OK?"

"Sure, why not?" I said, "we're both walnuts, right?"

We laughed.

I was also allowed to walk around the ward. The two telephones there were my saviour. Calling my friends up was the daily activity that I enjoyed most. I needed to connect myself with the outside world, to tell my friends of my solitary confinement, to ask for some understanding. Yet oftentimes, they didn't answer. Had my friends all gone to work? Or did they just refuse to talk to a nut like me? I called Phillip up every day, leaving messages on his voice mail, begging him to come to visit me. Yet days went by. There were no return calls, nor were there any visits from him either. Whenever the phone rang, I would be the first one to rush to answer it. I had become the chief operator for Bell Canada. When the calls were for another inmate, I became more disappointed than ever.

The daily staff meeting began promptly after breakfast and would last for about half an hour or so. Exciting, wasn't it? A gala event in this boring existence of ours, in this Haven of Hope. Like a group of devoted worshippers attending Sunday Service, doctors, nurses, social workers, and occupational therapists all gathered together in the common lounge of ward 9 South. They looked like relatives, mourning for a distant cous-

in in an exclusive funeral home at Forest Hills.

Not many deranged nuts such as myself enjoyed this daily ritual very much. Some would doze off while others would not pay any attention at all. Every day, John would be half asleep with his eyes staring blankly at a distance. Then there was Peter, who would always withdraw to a corner, playing monopoly. Yet no choice, perhaps. No staff meetings, no privileges. No privileges, no discharge. Day in, day out, same routine, same format. How different it was from the dynamic staff meetings that I had in my school when everyone participated. Worst of all, I was confused about the purpose of such meetings.

"Did you sleep well, Rosemary?"

No response.

"Fred, I'm surprised that you still smoke. You didn't smoke last week, did you?"

Only a nervous smile.

"Your husband came last night, right, Milly?"

A nod.

"Francis, you had a pass. How did it go? Would you like to share your visit with us?"

An embarrassing look.

"Who would clean the common lounge today? Nobody? Then, who would like to water the plant? No volunteer?"

"Well, Dr. Flak, do you want to make any comments?"

"Yes, I would like to thank everyone for coming to the meeting. The meeting is adjourned. Tomorrow, same time, same place. Have a good day," said Dr. Flak, jotting down some notes. He was the department head of 9 South. Carrying a knapsack most of the time, he seldom showed his empathy to inmates like me.

For these staff meetings, most of the time, silence. I didn't seem to hear any voice at all. Did it mean that I had been transferred to a Centre for the Deaf? Actually, the ritual of Holy Communion would be far more comforting and soul-searching. At least I could take the Bread and the Wine from the pastor and pray to God directly without fear.

On occasional days, there was a relaxation group for about half an hour. There were only a few inmates in the group, though.

"Now, listen to the relaxation music," said the occupational therapist as she turned on the tape. "Everybody, lie down on the floor. Close your eyes and imagine that you are at the beach. Twist your fingers, now your toes. Let go of your shoulders. That's it."

I didn't want to join. These relaxation exercises did not mean a thing to me. Yet what could I do? At least I had to appear to be cooperative to the nurses and the doctors. I would rather read a book, to divert my mind from thinking about Phillip. But there weren't any magazines or books around. Conformity without choice is a must in a mental institution.

On some evenings, there was a pet program in the lounge. A volunteer brought some puppies kept in a cage for us to talk to and pet. Why did I have to talk to a puppy and not Phillip? A puppy could not understand my feelings. Besides, I had always been afraid of animals. What was the purpose of having such a program? I did not know. When I looked at the puppies in the cage, I thought of us, inmates of the ward. After all, we were like "human puppies" kept in this mental cage, weren't we?

The baby grand piano in the lunchroom was a rare luxury in a mental institution. Yet there was no music program at all. Was the piano for show? Music has always been the best therapy for healing of all kinds, especially for mental patients like us. Once, I played Beethoven's *Moonlight Sonata* with another inmate, Wendy, looking on. Immediately, the doctor ordered me to stop. I was disturbing him in his meeting next door. I simply had to obey his order.

I wanted to make suggestions to the doctors about improving some of the programs. Yet could I? I didn't dare to make such an outrageous proposal. The doctors and nurses definitely knew more about psychiatry, hospital management, and humanity. Like a lot of

the inmates in this psychiatric ward, I was only a seriously ill patient who, in the eyes of these medical experts, was incapable of making any sound judgments or handling my own finances.

Like a herd of sheep following the shepherd on the way to see Christ on Christmas Day, I blindly walked behind the trail of doctors and nurses, hoping to see Christ and His Star. Yet I didn't see any stars at all. I didn't see any moon either. Not even a slight ray of the sun. How could I? Locked behind bars, without any hope for parole, hoping each day for a glimpse of the gray sky, for a breath of fresh air, and for just a bit of freedom to express my concerns to my loved ones.

Yes, I knew my limits. I could not fly beyond the comforts of this nest, this swallow's cage. I could not even escape, through the Gate of Hell, from this Holy Refuge.

All I could do was to remain a hostage of my captors in this Canadian mental institution. All I could do was to obey the rules of the hospital. Perhaps, one day soon, I would be able to break through this barrier of confined isolation, reach out to the bright blue sky, and proclaim to all my friends and neighbors, here and elsewhere, "Rejoice, Hallelujah! *I made it.*"

But, before then, *NO EXIT.*

Dear God,
Listen to my prayers,
Please.

Chapter five

The Lost World

One morning, at around six, the cries of one of my roommates, Carmen, awakened me. She was a middle-aged woman with long, sandy hair and a freckled face. Extremely skinny, her eyes seemed blank most of the time. She had been in the hospital since last week, but she hardly spoke. Every morning, she had trouble getting up for breakfast. Most days, she would just lie in her bed, staring at the ceiling, lost in a world of her own.

"What's the matter, Carmen?" I went over to her bed and asked.

"The doctor told me that I'll have to have electric shock treatment today."

"Why?"

"To treat my depression," she said, sobbing. "But I'm scared."

I gave her a tissue to wipe her tears. And I squeezed her hands to calm her down. What else could I do? I was only another inmate of the ward.

"Why are you depressed?"

"Well, probably, it's hereditary. When I was growing up, my mother suffered from depression. Just like what I am now—lying in bed all day, doing nothing, and unable to concentrate. Our house was a mess. My little sister was crying all day. I was only eight. But in those days, nobody knew the reasons why. My dad got so fed up with her that oftentimes he abused her physically after he got home, drunk. I lived in fear."

She stopped her reminiscing for a while. She seemed to have calmed down.

"When I was fourteen, I started drinking too. To escape from the miserable life I had at home. Then, at fifteen, I met my first boyfriend. He was cute with blonde hair. Very masculine too. We really had a great time together."

"Where did you meet your boyfriend?"

"At a nightclub. He was the bartender there. At seventeen, I became pregnant and had my baby. She looked exactly like my boyfriend. I named her Angela," she smiled at this moment. She showed me Angela's picture sitting at her bedside. Angela, about six, was indeed very pretty with big hazel eyes and lovely dimples.

"But my boyfriend left me. We were very young. He could not cope living with me and Angela crying all the time. I raised her alone. Now, she is about thirty-seven."

"Where is she now?"

"She lives in New York City."

"Does she know that you're in the hospital?"

"No. We're only in touch with each other occasionally."

I didn't dare to ask further about her relationship with her daughter. Was it the North American notion of independence and individualism that had made her relationship with her daughter distant? Or had her personal problems strained the relationship? My mother could never have stood me not being in touch with her. She called me up at least six times every day. When I was in the States, I received daily letters from her. I knew that Carmen, like my mother, loved her daughter very much. Yet perhaps there were different ways of expressing love? Or was it a cultural difference?

After taking a big breath, Carmen continued.

"I had several boyfriends afterwards, but none of them were like Angela's father. And in between, I was in and out of the hospital to treat my depression. I started living in a room in a boarding house after my discharge from my first hospitalization. The living conditions there were very bad. Made me more miserable and depressed than ever. I was lucky that I could afford to have a television. Everyday, I just sat in my room and watched television, doing nothing. The doctors gave me many medications—Prozac, Elavil, Paxil, and Zoloft. You name it, I've had it. But I'm still depressed. At times, I have been suicidal."

"You mean you thought of killing yourself?"

"Yes. At one time, I was on the subway platform. There was a voice in my head, telling me to jump on to the track. Then, I thought of Angela. She saved me."

Suicidal? I had never heard that depression could cause suicides. My thoughts went back to Hong Kong when I was in Grade Six. My godfather committed suicide by jumping from the ninth floor of a building. No one in his family could understand the reasons for his sudden death. Perhaps my godfather had suffered from bouts of depression that had been ignored and undetected.

"That's why the doctors here suggested that I have electric shock treatment," Carmen continued. "They say that it will lift my depression, but I'm frightened by the idea."

"Why?"

"My doctor showed me a short movie of this woman having the treatment. The doctors had to anesthetize the woman, give her a muscle relaxant, and then put that high voltage current pulse to her temples. They even had to put a wire in her mouth to bite. It's so gruesome and barbaric!"

"Then why did you consent to this kind of treatment?"

"Because the doctor told me that it is the last resort. Otherwise, I will have to be institutionalized forever. He told me that all I need is six weeks with three shock treatments every week. Then, I will feel better," she paused again and looked at me. "I don't know why I am confiding my problems to you all of a sudden. But I feel much better now. At least you listen." She gave me a big smile as if to say thank you.

"Don't mention it. I'm also sick, you know. We're in the same boat, right? I sure can understand how you feel. Just be brave and trust what the doctor tells you."

I gave her a comforting pat on her shoulder. She nodded her head. Then, she closed her eyes again, contemplative and lost in her thoughts.

At the back of my mind, I was worried about the side effects of elec-

tric shock treatment on Carmen. I had heard many stories from patients who had had this kind of treatment. They lost their memories. And many suffered from social isolation. I remembered my two favorite writers, Ernest Hemingway and Sylvia Plath. Both of them had adverse effects from such treatments. Ernest Hemingway shot himself because he could not bear having a void mind after the treatment. Sylvia Plath committed suicide. But of course, I did not tell Carmen about it.

After breakfast, I went into my room. Two nurses were there to put Carmen on a stretcher to go to the electric shock treatment room. Carmen looked at me, as if begging me to relieve her from her torment. Like a lamb about to be slaughtered, she could only submit to the nurses without offering any resistance. Yet I knew that, at the bottom of her heart, she was crying silently in desperation.

"Don't worry. You'll be alright," said Nurse Doreen in her professional tone of voice.

"Caroline," said Carmen. "Pray for me, will you?"

"Sure, I will."

She then gave me a faint smile.

Noontime came. The door of 9 South suddenly opened. Carmen was on the stretcher: her face white, her body motionless, and saliva dripping from her mouth. She looked like a living corpse. Only her toes twitched a tiny bit. What had become of her?

I did not go out to the lunchroom to have lunch that day. Just sat by Carmen's bedside. Disturbed by what I had seen, I became lost in my own thoughts about psychiatric treatments.

Was this invasive electric shock treatment the only solution for Carmen's depression? How about providing her with better psychotherapy sessions? Give her some hope, something to look forward to, a dream in her life? Solve her strained relationship with her daughter? Help her with better diet and coping skills? And teach her stress management strategies?

Carmen woke up after a while. I went to see her.

"Carmen, this is Caroline. Remember me?"

"Who?" She whispered.

"Your roommate, Caroline."

She did not respond. Her eyes just gazed out at a distance, trapped in her own world.

"Do you know where you are now?"

She turned her head towards me. Blankly she looked at me again.

"No. Where am I?"

"You're in Mount Sinai Hospital. Don't you remember?"

"Oh, yeah?"

I showed her Angela's picture. She looked at it, wanted to say something, but was hesitant.

"Who's this girl?" She asked, unable to comprehend.

"She's your little girl, Angela."

She did not respond. Just kept looking at the picture. Tears slowly came to her eyes.

In my heart, I cried too. Who wouldn't? Just a moment ago, she was alert and could engage in a conversation. Now, her mind had become empty, remembering nothing.

Could this kind of psychiatric treatment really help her overcome her depression? Even if it could, at what cost? To wipe out her memory? To create a void in her mind? But again, I was only another inmate, a layman in the field of psychiatry. I could not make any suggestions to the psychiatrists about their treatment of Carmen. All I could do was to pray to God that, one day, Carmen's memory would be restored and she would not have to live in the tormented state of depression again.

For the next six weeks, every Monday, Wednesday, and Friday, at around eight, Carmen had to go through this torturous treatment. Every time afterwards, she would seem half dead. And worse still, her memory deteriorated. There were times when she would mistakenly walk into

another inmate's room. Yet to me, she did not appear less depressed. She would still lie in her bed, gazing aimlessly at the ceiling most of the time. Worse still, when I tried to talk to her, she would not respond. She would just give me a faint smile. She did not challenge the nurses either. How could she? Everyday, she would just take the medications from the nurses obediently without resistance.

Then came one weekend after I returned from my pass. I found that Carmen's bed was empty. Surprised, I asked Nurse Doreen. Reluctantly, Nurse Doreen told me that the doctor had decided to send Carmen to Whitby Psychiatric Centre, a long-term mental institution outside of Toronto.

"Why?" I asked.

"The doctor thinks that she would be better taken care of there. She would be safer there. Besides, she doesn't have any relatives in Toronto," said Nurse Doreen. "Oh, by the way, she left something for you."

Nurse Doreen gave it to me. It was the picture of her little girl, Angela. Why did she give her beloved daughter's picture to me? Was it because she could not remember who she was? Or was it simply that she wanted to forget her past, now that she was going to be kept in a mental institution miles away from Toronto? Or was it that she hoped that I would be able to connect her with her daughter?

Had the doctor not told her once that with electric shock treatment, she would not be institutionalized, that her depression would get better? What had happened? But of course, I did not dare to ask Nurse Doreen. Maybe even she did not know.

I wanted to cry, but had to suppress my emotion in front of Nurse Doreen. She might think that I was getting disturbed if I cried. Then, she might ask the doctor to give me more tranquilizers. What if it was my turn to have electric shock treatment?

Calmly I went back to my room, buried my head in my pillows, and cried into them alone.

Outside, the sky was gray. Rain had been falling since the morning.

When the raindrops hit the windowpane, I could see Carmen, her skinny body, and her faint smiles. Yet I knew that I would never see her again. She had been lost inside the world of the mental health system. And she would probably be lost forever in a world of her own.

Dear God,
Help us,
Patients of mental institutions,
Please.

Chapter six

A WORLD OF HIS OWN

There was an empty bed in my room after Carmen left. Jen was my only roommate.

One evening after dinner, Jen and I were in our room. She was drinking her tea and I was writing my Chinese poems.

All of a sudden, an elderly man wandered into our room. His skinny, emaciated face made him look as if he were eighty years old. He seemed to be lost. He sat in the empty bed for a while, gazing into the distance. Then, he went to the washroom without closing the door. Scared, we pressed the button and called the nurse. Nurse Pat came.

"What's the matter, Collin? Can't you remember your room number?" Said Nurse Pat.

Collin looked at Nurse Pat. His eyes did not focus on her. Confused, he did not seem to understand the question.

"What's your room number, Collin?"

"Room 901."

"No, your room is Room 910. This is not your room."

"What's the number?" He asked, as if he were a little boy asking his mother for help.

"This room is 912. Come on, let's go. Leave the ladies alone," said nurse Pat, holding on to his hand.

"No, this is my room. See, that's my bed. And my shoes too," he insisted, refusing to leave.

"Be nice, Collin. Let's go to the lounge now and have your favorite apple juice. How about that?" Coaxed Nurse Pat.

Like a boy who had been awarded a prize, he nodded his head and followed Nurse Pat down the hall.

"What's wrong with him?" I asked Jen.

"Suffers from Alzheimer's Disease."

"How old is he?"

"I believe that he is about sixty years old at the most."

"But he looks as if he were in his eighties. Are you sure that he is only sixty years old?"

"I'm positive about his age. You see, his wife and daughters visited him the other day and I was in the lounge. His wife told me that they got married when he was fifty years old and they had twin daughters the year after. The daughters are just about nine."

"He's too young to have Alzheimer's. I thought that Alzheimer's only hit the oldies."

"It's not true. Alzheimer's usually hits people who are sixty or over."

"You're talking like a doctor, Jen. How do you know?"

"'Cause my grandmother suffered from Alzheimer's before she passed away in Taiwan, except that, in those days, we did not know its symptoms."

"What did your grandmother do?"

"Well, I was little then, but I still remember. She used to be very gentle and calm when I was four. But later, when I was six, her temperament changed. She started to be aggressive and would lose her temper very often, especially with my mother. Boy, my mother really suffered. You know how Chinese daughters-in-law are supposed to be, right? They have to be submissive to their mothers-in-law. Anyway, by the time I was eight, my grandmother started to be forgetful. She could not remember where she put her purse and started accusing my mother of stealing it from her. At times, she would kneel at the end of her bed, crying uncontrollably. There were days when she would just sit on the chair, gazing into the distance, without responding, just like Collin."

"Did you take her to see the doctor?"

"We didn't. We just assumed that it was old age. She was only seventy-one then. But one day, she left home without letting us know and wandered to an amusement park on her own."

"Did you call the police then?"

"Sure, we did. The police found her sitting in the park, holding a doll. When the police brought her home, she told us that she was fine and had not left home. It was after this incident that we took her to the doctor. The doctor diagnosed her as having Alzheimer's Disease."

"What happened afterwards?"

"The doctor gave her some pills to take, only to stabilize her, but would not cure her. Later, by the time I was ten, she could not comb her hair, nor could she brush her teeth. She had become incontinent too. My mother had to take care of her. And my mother hated it. She complained to my father and, of course, my father did not understand the emotional burden that my mother had to bear. So, day in and day out, my mother and my father fought. It was hell for me too!"

"Why didn't your parents send your grandmother to a nursing home?"

"You know the Chinese attitude towards the elders, especially in my father's generation. The son is obligated to take care of his parents. If you send your parents to a nursing home, it means that you don't respect them. The relatives would think that you are not a good and loyal son. A loss of face to the family, that is."

"Gee, that's hard on your mother and the whole family too. How old were you when your grandmother passed away?"

"I was fourteen. She died from falling onto the floor of the living room. One day, she was in one of her agitated moods. She wanted to leave the apartment on her own. As she was rushing to the door, she fell. That was it. We took her to the hospital. She even had an operation for her broken hip. But she didn't make it."

"Were you sad that she died, Jen?"

"In a way, yes, and in a way, no. You see, she was very kind to me before she became ill. I still have the little toy puppy that she bought for me when I started kindergarten. But it was the illness that robbed her of her mind. So it was sad. We just thought that it was her old age.

Had we known more about the symptoms of Alzheimer's, we could have taken her to see the doctors earlier. But from another perspective, it was nice that she died. We all have to die one day. She did not have to suffer anymore. And my mother was freed from the obligations and the responsibilities of having to look after my grandmother. There is peace and quiet back in our household again."

"I hope that I don't die of Alzheimer's. I'm single and have no kids. Who will look after me then?"

"Don't worry, Caroline. In Canada, even Chinese seniors with kids go to live in nursing homes now. Things have changed. Maybe you won't live that long, right? Just kidding!"

"You're right. Well, it is about time to have dinner now. Let's go and see what's on the menu today."

When we were at the dinner table, Collin sat opposite us. He had a napkin tied to his neck and a nursing assistant was spoon-feeding him.

"What's your name?" He asked the nursing assistant.

"Joyce."

"Oh," he answered. Then, his eyes gazed at a far corner. He seemed to have retreated into a world of his own. "When I was young, I was the chairman of World Vision. I have been to many of those underdeveloped countries: Columbia, Bangladesh, Haiti, and Guatemala. You should see those poor hungry children." He paused. His eyes became red and he did not seem to be able to control his emotions.

"Come, Collin, don't worry. That is all in the past," consoled Joyce.

"Well, I remember a whole bunch of kids, about four or five, sitting outside the office of the Canadian Embassy. When I went out of the Embassy, they were begging for money. Their eyes looked empty and stale," he continued. Now, he had tears in his eyes.

"It's OK," said Joyce. "You're now in Canada, Collin."

"No, I'm not. I am in Columbia."

Joyce wanted to laugh, but had to control herself. She probably knew

of his confusion, a typical symptom of Alzheimer's patients.

"Fine. You're in Columbia now. Why don't you eat the chicken? I've cut it up for you. Don't talk. Open your mouth. There you are. Good."

Piece by piece, Joyce patiently fed him.

"What did you just eat, Collin?"

"Fish," he answered without hesitation.

"What's my name, Collin?" Asked Joyce.

"Susan."

Joyce grinned.

"Who am I, Collin?"

Collin looked at Joyce's face for a while, as if searching for some familiar clues.

"You're my wife, Susan," he answered with a big smile.

"Well, don't worry. Whatever." Joyce did not argue with Collin. There was no point arguing with him. It would just worsen his agitation.

Collin started to talk to us.

"Well, ladies. Do you know that I was the chairman of World Vision? I have been to many of those underdeveloped countries: Columbia, Bangladesh, and Guatemala. You should see those poor hungry children. Well, I remember a bunch of kids, about four or five, sitting outside of the Canadian Embassy," he said.

"It's fine, Collin. It's about time for me to comb your hair in your room now. Let's go."

Collin looked at us.

"Good-bye, my dear daughters."

He waved at us. Unwillingly, he followed Joyce to his room.

Collin amazed me. He struck me as a compassionate person, in spite of his illness. Though he was apparently confused, he could still remember his younger days.

"See, Caroline, the way Collin repeats himself? That is another symptom of Alzheimer's Disease," said Jen.

"Did your grandmother do the same?"

"Of course. Everyday, she would tell us about her married life in China with my grandfather, the poverty in China in those days, and her escape to Taiwan."

"How did you and your parents react to her constant repetitions?"

"We got used to it. For me, I just took it with a grain of salt. Treat her as a music box. Sometimes, I would just close my bedroom door and ignore her."

At that moment, Collin's wife and his twin daughters came. His wife was in her mid-forties with short brownish hair. She had a bag of fruits. His daughters were very cute, but shy.

"Where is Collin?" Asked his wife to Jen.

"The nursing assistant has just taken him to his room to comb his hair."

"Thanks. By the way, my name is Susan and these are my daughters, Barbara and Bonnie. And you?"

"I'm Caroline."

"Nice to meet you. Barbara and Bonnie, do you want to go and see Dad? I've some fruits for him."

They looked at each other. Hesitantly, Barbara answered, "It's OK. Maybe later."

Susan went to the room, leaving Barbara and Bonnie in the dining lounge with us.

"Why don't you want to see your Dad?" I asked.

"He wouldn't know who we are anyway," Bonnie said.

I looked at them. They were playing with their Barbie dolls, giggling in a world of their own. They were too young to share the frustrations of their mother. Did they understand the deteriorating health of their father?

I thought of the agony of my mother. Perhaps, just like Barbara and Bonnie, I had never realized the anguish of my mother in having to take care of me when I was hospitalized. There was no professional support to help my mother with her fears, to help her understand more about the nature of my illness, nor were there any comforting words to help her overcome her anxiety.

"Barbara and Bonnie, let's go," said Susan as she came out of Collin's room. "I won't be seeing you two tomorrow."

"Why?" Asked Jen.

"Collin will be moving to the Baycrest Centre for Geriatric Care on Bathurst Street. He will be staying at the Apotex Centre, Jewish Home for the Aged, where they provide twenty-four hour care for Alzheimer's patients like him. They also have a good support system for caregivers. I will be less burdened and can pay more attention to the kids."

"All the best then. And take care," said Jen and I.

"I will. You too."

Barbara and Bonnie were bouncing back and forth as they followed their mother out the door. Childhood innocence without any worries. Their father was left in his room, reminiscing about his past, alone in a world of his own.

Dear God,
Help us in our agony,
Please.

Chapter seven

The Three Musketeers

At the left side of the ward is a small smoking room, the only "private" room for inmates to gather for a chat or two, to exchange information, and to support one another. Inmates would sit in there, each holding a cigarette. Though I was not a smoker, I found it a safe refuge for me to get away from the nurses. The air in the smoking room was filthy. Cigarette butts were lying on the ashtrays. Still, it was better than having to sit aimlessly in the lounge outside alone. At least there was some company.

There were three regulars in the smoking room—Tricia, Fred, and me. Tricia was about my age and was born in Boston. A bit older than me, Fred had a beard and a big stomach. He was a French Canadian from Montreal but had lived in Toronto since he was divorced from his wife twenty years ago.

We, the Three Musketeers, had become comrades in this Concentration Camp. Every evening, after dinner, we would gather together in this room and chitchat. Our gathering here was more fruitful and enjoyable than the staff meetings that we were obliged to attend every morning. We shared one thing in common—that is, we had all been diagnosed as manic-depressives.

"Tricia, is anyone in your family manic-depressive?" I asked.

"Yes, my father. There were days when he did not sleep at all. Then, his mood changed and became extremely hyper and agitated, yelling loudly at my mother and me. During one of his episodes, he lost a lot of money in his investments."

"That's what happened to me too," said Fred. "See, I lost a lot of money in the stock market when I was in my manic phase. That's why my wife left me. Afterwards, I was in a serious bout of depression. So there you are, one thing leads to another. A vicious circle, that is. How about you, Caroline?"

"Well, I don't know. As far as I know, none of my parents had been hospitalized for mental illnesses. But maybe, in Hong Kong, the symptoms were not detected. I just know that my father had a temper and my mother was very anxious all the time."

"What were you like when you were in your manic phase?"

"Just talked miles per minute and rambled on. Like a chatterbox. But I always talk fast in Chinese. And you, Tricia?" I asked.

Tricia was embarrassed. She looked at Fred. Then, she whispered to me.

"I became horny and wanted to make love. I also became excessively talkative. And I tended to buy expensive stuff too. I was in debt with my credit card. Now, I have a Public Trustee to look after my finances for me."

"Do you like the idea?"

"I certainly don't. But what can I do? At least I won't be in debt," said Tricia and shrugged her shoulders. She then got a cigarette out, asked Fred for a lighter, and continued.

I was surprised. I never had these symptoms.

"What triggered my manic-depression in the first place was my father. He physically abused me whenever he was in his high mood. He got drunk, came home, staggering, and beat me up if I did not listen to him. *I hate him!*"

Fred was silent. So was I. We sat there, listening to Tricia.

"If my father did not have manic-depression, I would not be here. I must be his scapegoat!" Her voice became louder, her speech more jabbered than ever.

"Are you alright?" Asked Fred, concerned.

"I'm fine. I'm going to get a glass of water. I'll be back."

Fred and I were left alone in the smoking room. Fred puffed his cigarette.

"Tricia always seems agitated whenever she talks about her father,"

said Fred.

"I know."

Silence again. Fred was lost in memory.

"What are you thinking, Fred?"

"Well, about my life and my illness. When I was diagnosed as a manic-depressive, I was about twenty-seven and newly married. Maybe it was the stress of marriage that triggered it. I still don't know the reason for it. My wife did not understand about my illness at all. I don't blame her for getting disappointed, especially for a newlywed. Our relationship became rocky. Then, I started smoking as an escape. She couldn't stand the smell of the cigarettes. I also looked for excitement. So I invested my money into the stock market. I lost it all in two days. She couldn't take it and left with our daughter."

"What happened afterwards?"

"I was depressed and had to be hospitalized here. Thanks to the social worker, I am now living in Supportive Housing close to downtown. I'm happy that I have my own place and my kitchen. And I get money from the Ontario Disability Support Program. That's good."

"Do you see your daughter?"

"Sometimes. She is a big girl now. Almost eighteen. She has her own life," he said with a sigh as if he regretted not being able to make up with his daughter when she was young. "You know what I do these days? I've joined the Mood Disorders Association of Ontario and Toronto, just to get some support and to make some friends. I go to their library to read books very often. Sometimes I help out in their office too. I also go to Progress Place downtown to work with my computer, to get a decent cheap lunch there, and to socialize with other survivors too."

"Then, why are you here now?"

"My mother passed away of lung cancer about two months ago. We were very close, especially since my wife left me. I couldn't handle it. I became depressed. Couldn't sleep at night. Lost my interest in life. Didn't even go to the Mood Disorders Association or Progress Place. All

of a sudden, life seemed so worthless. So I signed myself in voluntarily."

"When will you be getting out?"

"It depends on when the social worker will be able to arrange a mental health nurse from St. Elizabeth Health Care to see me once a week after discharge. How about you?"

"I don't know. Mine is an involuntary admission. It's up to the doctor," I said.

Tricia came back with a glass of icy cold water. She seemed to have calmed down and was in good spirits.

"Guys, don't complain too much now. Let's think of our future and our dreams. What do you want to do when you get out of here, Caroline?"

"To write a book about us and this place."

"Don't say this to the psychiatrists. They may take your aspiration as grandiose thought. Then, you will be here longer. Remember, grandiose thought is a symptom of manic state."

"Don't worry. You're not a psychiatrist. You can't lock me up. We are just prisoners of war here, all locked up already behind bars, right?"

Both Tricia and Fred laughed.

"Can't you see that a lot of writers are manic-depressives? I would just love to be one of those writers. How about you, Tricia?" I asked.

"To travel to the Caribbean and find a rich man to get married to!"

"You'd better watch out too. The doctor may take it as another grandiose thought too. Poor judgment, they would say."

"Can't they see that we are also human beings who need a fulfilled life with love? Well, this is just an impossible dream. Perhaps it's just something for me to daydream about in my boring life. How can I have enough money to go to the Caribbean when the Public Trustee controls my finance?" Said Tricia. "And you, Fred, how about you?"

"To look for a job in my field."

"What's your field?"

"An art teacher. I graduated from the Fine Arts Department of York

University. And I also have an Art Therapy Certificate. I was teaching art to the seniors in a nursing home before I became sick."

"That's a very lofty idea," I said, "I know that the Canadian Mental Health Association might have jobs in this field. But I think that you'll have to do some volunteer work for them first."

"Doesn't matter. I hope to have my job as an art therapist back one day. If there is a will, there is a way. But first, get well."

"Wow! Here we are, the Three Musketeers of Concentration Camp 9 South. Caroline will be a writer one day, Fred's going to be an art therapist, and I'll be the wife of a millionaire!"

There was a knock at the door. In came Nurse Marilyn.

"Guys, it's getting late now. It's about time for your medications. Go to the front counter and I'll give them to you."

The Three Musketeers had to leave their sanctuary. All at once, we became three devoted pilgrims, silently following behind Nurse Marilyn. Obediently at the counter, we took our medications. Afterwards, we went back to our rooms, dreaming of our dreams, hoping that they will be true one day.

Dear God,
Would our dreams
Come true one day?
Tell us, please.

Chapter eight

Let Us Go Then

"Lin, this is Shiu-Ching. I've got some bad news. Dr. Wong just called and told me that Caroline is in the hospital again."

"Again? How could that be? She seemed to be fine when I saw her about two months ago."

"Maybe it has to do with the problem with her boyfriend Phillip. Dr. Wong did not say much about it on the phone. I have always told her that Phillip is not trustworthy. Probably this break-up has triggered her manic-depression again. I've told her a million times not to go out with men. One can survive very well without them. But she doesn't listen to me. You know that daughters don't listen to their mothers."

"I know. 'Cause daughters and mothers are both women. And, as always, there is a generation gap."

"That Phillip had a lot of girlfriends before. And he is not as bright as Caroline. Besides, he is not Chinese. Dr. Wong also told me that the principal of the school had kindly asked Caroline to go home and rest for a few days. See, Lin, her problem is that she is very stubborn and rebellious at times. When she was a child, she would sit if you told her to stand. After her studies in the States, she became very independent. I'm afraid that she may have the same problem with her principal. Or she forgot to take her medications. You know, Lin, every day, I would call her up to remind her to take the medications. Medications are very important for her illness. She just ignores me and sees my concerns as nagging and probing into her private life. I'm her mother after all. I just want to protect her from getting sick again. You know how some people despise this kind of mental illness."

"Don't let those ignorant people bother you, Shiu-Ching. Everything will be fine. Let's put all our worries in God's hands."

"It's easier said than done. I'm worried about if she will be allowed to teach again. See, teaching is her passion. What if she cannot teach? What will happen to her?"

"Don't imagine things. The Toronto District School Board has a very good disability pension plan. If worst comes to worst, she can always apply for it. After all, did you not tell me that she has been contributing to the plan every month ever since she started teaching with the board? She can survive. She is bright and determined."

"Lin, I don't speak English. But I would like to talk to the doctor in the hospital."

"It's alright. I can go with you. Don't forget that I was a pharmacist in one of the psychiatric institutions in Hong Kong before coming to Canada. At least, I can speak English and understand some of the medical terms."

"That would be perfect."

"Just stay calm and don't panic. Hospitals are meant to help people to become healthy. See, even a car needs a tune-up sometimes. Why not a human being? Caroline is extremely intelligent. With the help of the medical staff and medications, she will get over it and be fine again."

"I know. Lin, why don't we meet after church, have our lunch at McDonald's and visit Caroline at Mount Sinai Hospital afterwards?"

"That's good. We had better stop now and I'll see you after church."

After Shiu-Ching had finished talking to Lin, she began to cry. She didn't even cry when her husband passed away of a heart attack in 1984. Did it mean that she didn't love her husband? Or did it mean that she reflected an era when Chinese women had to suppress their emotions, showing no expressions of love or hate?

Tolerance, to Shiu-Ching, was a virtue. So was obedience. Her inner pride forbade her to cry. Could it be that in her mind, crying was a sign of being a fragile Chinese jade locked behind a glass cupboard for people to comment on and to pity? Dignity and respect were what she wanted to have. Yet now, for once, she had to let go of her frustrations.

She had brought Caroline up to the best of her ability—gave her piano lessons, took her to concerts, hired an amah, and sent her to one of the best schools. These "luxuries" were rare in Hong Kong in the fifties. She even used her own savings to send Caroline to study in the States. What more could she have done?

But now, Caroline was diagnosed as a manic-depressive—a psychiatric disease that many Chinese looked down upon and could not understand. She could not understand either. Why her beloved daughter Caroline? She would be more than willing to have the illness herself and spare Caroline. Yet what could she do? God's will? Or Satan's curse? Was she, as a mother, responsible for this hereditary disease? Was she responsible for not teaching Caroline how to cope with emotional encounters with men? Or was Caroline a scapegoat of the competitive educational system in Hong Kong? Or is it simply that, as new Canadians, both she and Caroline did not understand the hospital system in Canada, the prescribed medications, and the rights of the mentally ill? Just like Caroline, her mind was tormented with anguish.

Who could understand her frustrations, her inner agony, her helplessness? Who could comfort this eighty-one year old woman, who cannot understand English, yet has to live in an English-speaking environment? Nobody. Guilt and fears mingled in her heart. How could she be of help to her daughter? She didn't know.

Slowly she took the Bible out from her drawer and sat on her bed in her barely decorated apartment. She turned to the Old Testament with her frail hands. Quietly she read *Psalm Twenty-Three* aloud:

"The Lord is my shepherd,
I shall lack nothing.
He makes me lie down in green pastures,
He leads me beside quiet waters,
He restores my soul.
He guides me in paths of righteousness
for His name's sake.

> *Even though I walk through the valley*
> *of the shadow of death,*
> *I will fear no evil,*
> *for you are with me.*
> *Your rod and your staff,*
> *they comfort me…"*

Just like Virgin Mary holding Jesus Christ after the crucifixion, Shiu-Ching held her daughter's picture, cried aloud, and prayed to God in despair and desolation.

She looked at the clock. It was about ten now. Well, time to go to the Toronto Chinese Baptist Church in Chinatown. Gently she wiped away her tears and dressed in her traditional Chinese costume. She looked in the mirror. She noticed her wrinkled face. She was getting old. Who would look after Caroline after she died? She was worried, but managed to put on a smile. A smile that hid her inner pain and anguish. In short, a human mask.

Hurriedly, she took the subway at the Eglinton Subway Station. Sitting across from her in the subway train was a Chinese woman of about forty and her little girl. The little girl, about four, had a pigtail and a pair of glasses. All at once, Shiu-Ching thought of Caroline. Caroline's birth, though a difficult one, was a joy to her. After all, she had had several miscarriages before Caroline. Caroline was her jewel and her pride. She could not afford to lose her. When Caroline had her bouts of fever as a baby, she would have sleepless nights, worrying. Just like this little girl, Caroline had to wear glasses to correct her cross-eyed vision. Every day until Caroline was in Grade Ten, she had to ask Amah Hing to take Caroline to school. She would insist that Caroline not have any boyfriends, but rather, concentrate on her studies. She wanted Caroline to be a success. To her, Caroline was a success, having finished university within a short time. In all the letters that Caroline wrote to her when she was

studying in the States, she never asked for money. It was after Caroline's return to Hong Kong that she learned that Caroline had been doing several odd jobs at the same time. She was delighted and proud to have such a good daughter. But could it be that Caroline was over-worked, that she became emotionally fragile, which led to this manic-depression?

"Mama, I'm tired," said the little girl, leaning onto her mother's lap.

Her mother touched and hugged her fondly.

As Shiu-Ching looked on, she wished that when Caroline was little, she could have done the same as this Chinese woman. But regrettably, she hadn't. Why? It was unthinkable for Chinese parents in her time to express their love for their children this way. To hide one's emotions and love was a virtue. Yet would it be too late for her to hug Caroline now?

Shiu-Ching got off at the St. Patrick Subway Station, walked a few blocks to Beverley Street, and arrived at the church just in time. Reverend Wong gave a sermon on Jesus' healing.

"In Mathew Chapter Eight, verses two to three, it says that a man with leprosy came and knelt before Jesus and said, 'Lord, if you are willing, you can make me clean.' Jesus reached out his hand and touched the man. 'I am willing,' he said. 'Be clean.' Immediately he was cured of his leprosy…"

Shiu-Ching fervently prayed to God. If Jesus could heal a leper whose illness, the same as mental illness, was despised by others, He could definitely heal Caroline. After her prayer, she felt that one day God would set Caroline free of her torment.

Reverend Wong concluded his sermon. "Mathew Chapter Six says, 'look at the birds of the air; they do not sow or reap or store away in barns, and yet your heavenly Father feeds them. Are you not much more valuable than they? Therefore do not worry about tomorrow, for tomorrow will worry about itself. Each day has enough trouble of its own."

Yes, she should not worry too much about Caroline's health. Shiu-Ching felt consoled and comforted by God's words. After all, Caroline was lucky that she was in one of the best hospitals in Toronto.

She met Lin after church. Shiu-Ching was about five feet and weighed only eighty-five pounds. Her wrinkled face looked pale, her veins stood out in her frail arms.

When she came to Canada some twenty years ago, she was radiant. Was it her inability to adjust to Canada that had made her aged? Or the death of her husband? Or the illness of Caroline that worried her? She was the beauty of the family. Her delicate hand-made cheong sam dresses, her gracious poise, her make-up, and her dimples were admired by everyone. Yet these days, she did not wear any make-up. Everyday, she wore the same dress and shoes. Why the change?

Holding each other's arms in the hot summer heat, supporting each other in their frail and fragile existence, Shiu-Ching and Lin went to eat at McDonald's. Lin, as tiny as Shiu-Ching, was a few years younger. She had graduated from the University of Hong Kong in the Department of Pharmacy. In her day, it was rare for a Chinese woman to have achieved this much.

Both ordered their favorite fish burgers and hot tea. Shiu-Ching, as always, insisted on paying.

"Let me pay. I owe you for going to the hospital with me, Lin."

"OK, Shiu-Ching. You're always so generous."

"Give me the bill, please," said Shiu-Ching to the server at the counter. That was one of the few sentences that she could say in English.

Lin and Shiu-Ching sat down. Shiu-Ching just had a bite of the fish burger.

"It doesn't taste good. I won't eat it," said Shiu-Ching.

"You have to eat, my friend. You're so stressed these days with your worries about Caroline. Did you have breakfast?"

Shiu-Ching did not reply.

"I bet that you didn't. Listen to me. Eat, OK?"

Unwillingly, Shiu-Ching had another big bite. She then drank her tea.

"Did you sleep well last night?" Asked Lin.

"I did with the sleeping pill."

"I did not know that you are taking sleeping pills. When did you start taking them?"

"Well, a long time ago. If I didn't take it, I would be imagining things. See, I have to have at least eight hours of sleep."

"I don't know about you. But oldies like us don't need eight hours of sleep. What kind of medication are you taking? Do you have it with you now? Let me take a look. I am a pharmacist, remember?"

Shiu-Ching took the medication out. Lin looked at it. It was risperidone. Lin knew that it was a major anti-psychotic neuroleptic medication. What was wrong with Shiu-Ching? Was she mentally ill too? Lin did not have the courage to ask.

"It's nice that you're here with me. Come to think of it, we've known each other for a long time," said Shiu-Ching.

"Yes, we knew each other when we were at the Baptist Church on Caine Road in Hong Kong. That was about fifty years ago, wasn't it? We were young then. Remember that Caroline was in the same room as my nephew when she had her tonsils removed?

"Of course, I remember. She used to be sick every week because of her tonsils. I was worried to death. That's why the doctor advised me to have her tonsils removed. It cost a lot of money then. He was a top-notched private surgeon in those days."

"She's fine now. Don't worry too much."

"I know. Do you know that I had her when I was thirty-seven? She is my consolation."

"I understand."

"After her divorce, I have had to protect her more. I don't want her to be involved in relationships. See, men are not trustworthy and would probably cheat on her. But she wouldn't listen to me. She had been hurt by her husband before, but in 1992, she still went out with another man. She ended up sick afterwards. And now, another relationship and another relapse. I've told her that she is a manic-depressive and should not have any relationships with men," said Shiu-Ching, frustrated.

Paused for a while, she said, "I have to buy Caroline a vanilla milk-shake. That's her favourite."

Slowly she got her coins out and went to the counter to get the shake. Lin watched her. Lin could not quite agree with Shiu-Ching. She knew that the mentally ill are, like any other human beings, capable of love and needing to be loved, that they have their desires and needs. But she would not argue with Shiu-Ching.

Shiu-Ching came back with a big milkshake. They left McDonald's and arrived at the university entrance of the hospital. Up they went to 9 South, only to find that Caroline was fast asleep. Like a sleeping beauty she lay on her bed, probably dreaming of her Prince Charming giving her a kiss of true love.

Both Lin and Shiu-Ching waited at her bedside. Seeing that Caroline had lost some weight, Shiu-Ching's heart ached with pain. She could not help gently touching Caroline's hands. For once, she had broken through the tradition of withholding her emotions. Lin squeezed Shiu-Ching's hands and gave her a smile. And Lin quietly cited T. S. Eliot's poem, *The Love Song of J. Alfred Prufrock,* to herself:

"Let us go then, you and I,

When the evening is spread out

Against the sky.

Like a patient etherized

Upon a table,

Oh, do not ask what is it,

Let us go and make our visit."

Dear God,
Answer the mother's prayer,
Please.

Chapter nine

THE VISIT

As Shiu-Ching and Lin were about to sit down, a young nurse in her mid-twenties came into the room.

"My name is Jane. I'm sorry that you can't see Caroline. It's doctor's orders that she can't have any visitors today."

In her broken English, Shiu-Ching said, "Why? Me mother. Must see her."

"I understand, Mrs. Kwok. But it's doctor's orders. The doctor prefers Caroline to rest and not to be disturbed."

"No disturb. Sit by bedside. Watch her sleep. Want talk to doctor."

"I'm afraid you can't, Mrs. Kwok. The doctor is not in the ward now. You can sit in the lounge for a while if you want, but not in her room."

Reluctantly, these two ladies looked at each other and nodded their heads. Shiu-Ching touched Caroline's hands once again and left the milkshake by her bedside. They looked at Caroline, who seemed to respond to the visit, even though she was in a deep sleep. Perhaps she realized, in her sleep, the love and warmth of her mother and Auntie Chiu. Extra-sensory perception, we say? Or just pure spiritual communication?

There was no coffee in the lounge, nor was there any tea, except for an empty teapot by the refrigerator. Only a comfortable sofa for these two seniors to sit on. They looked around at the lounge. There were drawings on the wall. At one end was a drawing, freedom, with a bird singing in a forest. At the other end, there was a drawing of a lion and a mouse. There were some games on the shelf behind the sofa.

A young man in his twenties sat at the far end of the room, as if he were a monk praying in a monastery. Lanky with a beard, he had long brown hair hanging onto his shoulders. His dark-brown eyes gazed blankly. Quiet and subdued he was. A sign of depression? Or could it

be the result of medications? As laymen in the field of psychiatry, both Shiu-Ching and Lin thought that this young man was quite "normal."

"Why is it that he has to be in the hospital? He doesn't look as if he is crazy at all," asked Shiu-Ching.

"Yes, he doesn't seem to harm others. Just a loner, maybe," said Lin.

He came over and started to talk.

"My name is Reverend Cheung. What's your name?"

"I'm Lin and she's Shiu-Ching."

"Where are you from?"

"We're from Hong Kong," said Lin.

"Hong Kong? That's a British colony, right? It is a small island with lots of mountains in the South China Sea."

"That's right. Your geography is very good," said Lin.

"Yes, I was in my first year at the University of Toronto when I became ill. I like geography, history, and especially religion. I read a lot, except that these days, when I am in the hospital, there aren't any books for me to read."

Lin translated to Shiu-Ching in Chinese. Shiu-Ching was surprised that he was, like her daughter, a university student. Before Caroline became sick, she had not known that mental illness could hit every class, every race, and every intelligence level.

"How long have you two been in Canada?"

"Well, I have been here for about fifteen years and my friend has been here for over twenty years now," said Lin.

"That's a long time," he said. "So your friend has never learned English?"

"Never. One doesn't have to in Toronto."

"Why?"

"She speaks Chinese. In Toronto, there are many Chinese supermarkets and restaurants. There are also Chinese radio and television stations. Many Chinese whom I know have lived in Toronto for ages, but still don't know English. They can get by," said Lin. "How about you? You

must have been born in Canada."

"I was born in Winnipeg. My parents were divorced when I was ten. I then moved to Toronto with my mother and have been living here since," he paused for a while. "Do you hear voices?"

"No, I don't. Do you?" Asked Lin.

"Yes I do. I hear God's voice every day."

"What does God tell you?" Lin was curious.

"He told me that I am His son, Jesus, that I should go and spread the Gospel for Him. The world today is full of evils and I am chosen by God to save the world. Are you two Christians?"

"Yes, we are. Which church do you belong to?"

"Peoples' Church on Sheppard and Bayview. Let us bow our heads and pray together."

Both Lin and Shiu-Ching looked at each other, astonished and confused. How could this young man be Reverend Cheung? He did not look Chinese at all. And to call himself Jesus?

This young Reverend began to pray loudly, with both hands lifted high up.

"Lord, have mercy on us,
Lord, help us,
Lord, forgive our sins,
Lord, save us from evils,
Lord, restore our faith,
Lord, bless the world,
Amen."

His voice cracked and his eyes filled with tears. What an emotional religious plea!

But all of a sudden, the nurse came. Sternly, with her fingers pointing at him, she said, "Tom, stop shouting your prayer. Don't scare these two ladies. You are not Jesus. You're Tom Davey."

He protested in a loud voice.

"My name is *not* Tom Davey. My name is Jesus. I'm the Messiah and I am here to save this wretched world. This is my mission. Don't you know that you all have sins?" He then began to mumble.

"Stop it," said the nurse. "If you keep being agitated like this, I'll give you a shot or put you in restraints."

Tom did not listen. He just didn't seem to fear this threat. He kept on praying. Then, he began to preach as if he were Jesus Christ.

> *"Blessed are the poor in spirit,*
> *for their's is the kingdom of heaven.*
> *Blessed are those who mourn,*
> *for they will be comforted.*
> *Blessed are the meek,*
> *for they will inherit the earth."*

Both Lin and Shiu-Ching were amazed at the religious fervour of this young man, even though they hardly knew him. They were surprised by Tom's good memory of the Bible.

But within a few seconds, two nurses and two security guards came to the lounge, as if they were the Gang of Four during the Chinese Cultural Revolution. Tom was in terror.

"Oh, no. Don't do this to me again. I'll listen to you. Please don't give me the shot. I'll behave. I won't preach anymore."

Tom's plea for mercy really moved the two ladies.

"Nurse, it's OK. Let him preach. He didn't frighten us," said Lin.

"Don't worry, ladies. He does it all the time. We'll handle him," said one of the nurses. "Tom, you need to have a shot to calm you down, to get you out of your delusion."

Tom began to cry—a cry of helplessness, a cry of desperation. Even Lin and Shiu-Ching felt sorry for him. They could see tears rolling down his face.

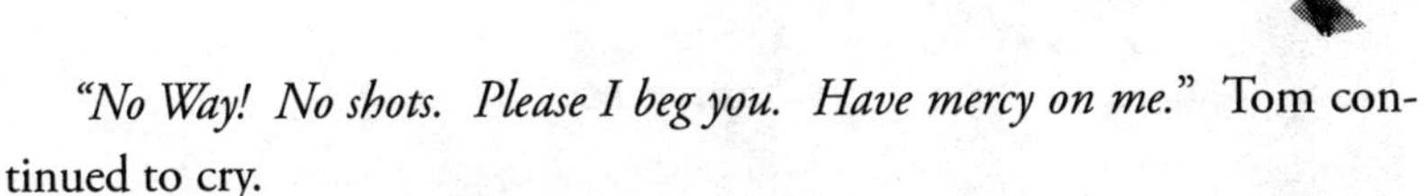

"No Way! No shots. Please I beg you. Have mercy on me." Tom continued to cry.

Yet there was no sympathetic response, nor was there a compassionate word of comfort from these nurses, let alone a pat on the shoulder. Look at this Gang of Four. Tightly they held Tom's arms, escorted him to his room, put him in the bed. Then, they gave Tom a needle.

Afterwards, the Gang of Four marched out of the room. Their mission was complete. Tom no longer cried. Shiu-Ching and Lin could not hear any more of his preaching either. Just like the drawing in the lounge, from a ferocious lion, Tom had become a tame mouse all at once.

Both Lin and Shiu-Ching were made apprehensive by this show of cruelty. No human touch at all. Shiu-Ching was worried.

"Lin, we'd better leave this place before another scene happens. I just hope that they will be nice to Caroline."

"Don't worry, Shiu-Ching. Caroline is in good hands. Yes, we had better go."

On their way out of the ward, they held hands, as if to say to the medical staff that, in unison and in spirit, they support the oppressed psychiatric patients not only at Mount Sinai, but all over the world.

Dear God,
Show Your Mercy
To these oppressed souls,
Please.

Chapter 10

ROLLER COASTER RIDES

As Shiu-Ching and Lin were about to leave the ward, there was a new admission. This time, a young woman was tied to the stretcher with two paramedics holding on to her. A chubby woman with long, dark hair and brown eyes, she was about thirty years old. Hysterically she yelled, "Let me go, let me go. I don't want to be here again. I want to see my little boy! Where is my son Tim? I want to see him!"

Nurse Natalie patiently talked to Anita.

"Calm down, Anita. Don't be so hyper. You're sick now. Once you get better, you'll see Tim."

Innocently, she looked at Nurse Natalie and seemed to believe her words without question. Yet within a few seconds, she began to cry again.

"Where is Tim? Where is Tim? I want to see my little Tim."

"Don't worry, Anita. Your little son is with your husband now. Once you are well, we'll ask your husband to bring him to see you."

"No! I don't want my husband. I want my son!"

"OK, that's fine. But first, you have to get better. Trust me. I'm your primary nurse, right? You remember me, don't you?"

Anita nodded her head. Yes, just about a year ago, she was in the same ward and Nurse Natalie was her nurse. Yes, she was diagnosed as a manic-depressive the last time she was here. She had been taking lithium and haloperidol ever since then. Once a skinny woman who weighed 110 pounds, she now weighed about 130 pounds. And her hands trembled too. *She hated those pills!*

"Now, I'll untie your strap and show you to your room. Here, put the hospital gown on. I'll give you the medications in a little while. They will make you feel better."

"I'm scared. Those medications make me feel like a zombie. What

if I die?"

"Don't be silly, Anita. You won't die. Just relax a bit now. We'll talk. Mount Sinai is one of the best hospitals in Canada. You'll be OK," assured Nurse Natalie with a smile. "Remember what you called it the last time you had a mood swing? You called it a roller coaster ride."

"Oh, yes. I remember now. After a few weeks, I was out of the hospital and I was able to take care of Tim."

"See? You can do it. I'll be back with the medications in a few minutes."

After Nurse Natalie had left, Anita went to the washroom. She held onto a cup with her trembling hands, filled it with water, drank it all, and then urinated. She had turned into a camel in the desert after she started taking the medications. Another side effect, the doctors say. She had also become lethargic and tired. She seemed to have lost her interests in her passion for music. Her only hope was her son, Tim.

Nurse Natalie came back with the medications.

"What are they?" Asked Anita.

"They're lithium, haloperidol, and clonazapam. You know that lithium stabilizes your mood. And haloperidol and clonazapam are tranquilizers to calm you down."

"But?"

"You want to see your son, right? So take them, OK?" Nurse Natalie gave her a smile again. "Come on, all the way down."

Anita took the medications and rested on her bed. Surprisingly, her hysterical mood seemed to have subsided. She was calm again. She thought of her son's birthday three years ago when she and her husband took him to Wonderland. For the first time, the three of them went on a roller coaster ride. She could still remember the thrills of the ride. Those were the happy times. But two years ago, her husband's accounting company laid him off. Though they had no problems financially with a good package from the company, her husband had lost his hope in finding a job after many rejections. Seeing her husband's frustrations made her worried too. She would nag her husband at times. He became temperamental and agitated. Worse still, he was hooked on alcohol, an escape from the cruel reality of unemployment. He would shout at her and Tim for no reason. At times, when he was drunk, he would hit her. This kind of abuse made her afraid of her own safety and her son's. She lived in fear and lost sleep. It caused her mood to become hyper, irritable, and she lost touch with reality. She saw her family physician who referred her to Mount Sinai Hospital a year ago.

"Anita, are you feeling better? Do you want to talk to me now or later?" Nurse Natalie's voice broke her train of thought.

"Oh, sure, now. Why not?"

"What do you want to talk to me about?"

"Well, about my marriage and my son. See, I love my husband and my son. But he would hit me after he got drunk. And these days, with the medications that I am on, he thinks that I am too fat and has been coming home late. We haven't had sex since I have been on those medications. Probably it is my fault too. Somehow, after I've been on those pills, I am not interested in having sex anymore," said Anita embarrassingly.

"Did you contact the police about his physical abuse?"

"No, I didn't dare."

"Why?"

"Cause the police would probably charge him and that would make the situation worse."

Nurse Natalie paused. Anita's story was not new to her. In her contacts with her woman patients, many seemed to have become mentally ill because of their husband's abuse or undetected marital problems.

"Why?"

"Don't forget that I'm a manic-depressive. See, after he had been laid off from work and my diagnosis, many of our relatives had already disassociated with us, except for my parents. What if he were in prison for hitting me? My parents would not forgive him. That would leave Tim

and me with no emotional support."

"Now I understand. Do you want me to arrange for a social worker to help you with your problems? She can contact a marriage counselor for you and your husband."

"I'll think about it. I like the idea, but it's just that my husband may not like it. See, men are generally pretty reserved about this topic, and he's especially so because he is from England."

"OK, we'll leave it later then. Why are you here this time?"

"Well," said Anita hesitantly. "I just…"

"Just what? Tell me."

"I haven't been taking my medications," confessed Anita.

"What?"

"Yes, for about a month now. I just have the bottles of pills sitting in my bathroom."

"Why?"

"Because I *hate* the hand tremors, the thirst, the weight gain, the dry mouth, and all the rest of it!"

"But you know that one can't just withdraw drastically from one's medications. Even with vitamins, one can't do that. See, Anita, had you not withdrawn from taking those medications, you would probably not be here. You would be with your son."

"Yes, I regret it now."

"You know what you should have done? You should have told your psychiatrist about the side effects. He could have changed the dosage or the medication for you."

"Yes, I should have. But what can I do now?"

"Nothing. Just relax and leave it to the doctors here. By the way, I remember that you were a chain smoker. Have you cut down your smoking a bit?"

"I have. I used to smoke four packs a day. But now, I only smoke one pack."

"That's a good sign. But you should cut it off to zero. It's no good for your lungs."

"I know. But see, I have been a chain smoker since I was fifteen. My father passed away that year of cancer. It was tough for a teenager to handle."

"I understand. But with determination, one can kick one's bad habit, right? Just think of your son Tim. You have to give him hope besides loving him. If you don't take care of your health, how can you give him hope in life?"

"That's right. I'll try."

"I think that I'll leave you alone now. Get some rest before dinner comes. I'll talk to you about getting you in touch with a support group later. Sometimes, it is peer support that can give some understanding and help because they are in the same boat as you, right?"

"Thanks so much, Nurse Natalie. You are one of the nicest nurses I've ever had."

"Thank you."

Nurse Natalie left Anita resting in her bed. She thought of suggesting to the psychiatrist switching Anita's lithium to epival, an anti-convulsant medication with fewer side effects. But would the psychiatrist listen to her suggestion, she wondered. She was only a young graduate nurse, new to the ward. She also thought of the Mood Disorders Association of Ontario and Toronto. Yes, she knew that the peer support groups and family workshops there could certainly give Anita some emotional support and help. After all, had she not got help from this Association when her own sister was diagnosed as a manic-depressive?

Dear God,
Give me strength,
And determination,
Please.

Chapter eleven

If I Had A Voice

I was sitting by the piano in the lunchroom when the door of 9 South opened. I saw my mother in her gray suit, carrying a big brown bag. Her emaciated face looked tense.

"Yeng, come and eat the barbecued duck that I got from Chinatown for you. It's fresh and tastes very good," she said, delighted to see me. She untied the bag with her hands. The veins in her skinny arms were distinct.

"It's fine, Mom. I just had my lunch. I bet that you haven't had your lunch. Why don't you eat?"

Disappointed, she said, "But I bought it especially for you."

"OK, then, why don't we eat it together?"

Happily she got the chopsticks out from the bag, laid the paper plates on the table, and took the barbecued duck out.

"Have you taken your medications? How do you feel today?" She asked. "Have some more duck. You've got to eat, Yeng. You're sick."

"You should eat more, Mom. You're so skinny," I said. She seemed to have lost some weight lately. I was worried about her health too. From the time I entered the hospital, she had been coming to visit me every day, bringing me Chinese food.

My illness must have tormented her mind. Being a loner, she did not have many friends except Auntie Chiu. She would not have confided her worries in others. She probably refused to tell others about my illness since it would have been considered a shame to the family. Or was it simply her personality to suppress her emotions? Or was she emotionally insecure?

Indeed, ever since I was a little girl, she had worried about my health. She would insist that I see a doctor even if I coughed just a little. After my father passed away, my divorce, and the diagnosis of my manic depression, her worries about me became more intense. I was overwhelmed by her concerns, but I could not blame her. After all, she suffered several miscarriages before she had me, so I was special to her. With my father always on business trips, my brother Bill and I were all she had.

"What are you reading now?" Asked my mother, noticing that I had a book.

"Well, just a novel that my friend Catherine gave to me."

"Didn't I always tell you not to read any novels? Those novels will only make your illness worse," she said, raising her voice. "Remember how you became ill when you were in Hong Kong after your graduation?"

I looked at my mother. I did not talk back. Why should I argue in the hospital? I would only be considered more manic if I did. There would probably be more tranquilizers. In fact, I had learned not to talk back to my mother after what had happened to me in 1973.

After graduating from school in the States in 1972, I went to Europe on my own for two months with a Eurailpass, staying in youth hostels. I visited many museums and Art Galleries and went to the Lake District where William Wordsworth lived. The adventures I experienced when traveling, the exposures to different cultures, and the freedom to see the world had changed me from a dependent, over-protected teenager into an independent young woman. Besides, my stay in Minneapolis as a foreign student had already exposed me to an academic culture that I found challenging and intellectually stimulating. The spacious, quiet living environment, the mixing with my American friends, the exposures to concerts and theatres, and the generosity of some of my professors had changed my value system and my attitude to learning. But of course, I missed Hong Kong, my friends, my parents, and my Amah Hing. I decided to return to Hong Kong to take a Diploma of Education at the University of Hong Kong, hoping to become a high school teacher there.

I must have suffered from cultural shock upon my return. The congested living environment appalled me. The trams, the cars, and the people! And the high rises too.

The campus at the University of Hong Kong was so small in comparison to the campus in Minnesota. In class, my classmates were so obedient that they seldom asked questions, as had my American classmates. My girlfriends from high school had never been abroad to study in those days, neither had they been to Europe. To them, I had been "Americanized." How could you, they said, have changed after living in the States for only two and a half years? How come your English accent had become so different from us? They did not understand my frustrations in the States and the loneliness of being a foreign student. They did not understand the many odd jobs that I had in the States. I felt ostracized in Hong Kong, unable to communicate with my friends in this city of my birth. After all, had I not always wanted to return to Hong Kong in order to blend in with my Chinese culture once again, to acquaint myself with my friends, and to change the educational system in Hong Kong?

Yet once again, just like years ago, I had to live in an over-protected environment. Amah Hing prepared my underwear and turned on the shower for me every day. Though I did not like the idea, I could not refuse. They had missed me and they loved me. My parents could not understand what appeared to them to be my new behaviour. "Why do you always have to sit on the floor with a bottle of coke? You weren't like this before," my mother would say. They could not accept the fact that I had grown up and changed.

Besides taking the Education course, I also had a job teaching English as a Second Language at the Language Centre of the university. I found my teaching there extremely satisfying. I was proud that I could be a tutor at the most prestigious university in Hong Kong. What I had learned in the States allowed me to help my Chinese students. My boss, Bob Lord, was a British professor from Liverpool. He was the only person with whom I could really communicate at the time. I felt that he could

understand me best. I talked to him about my professional dreams, my frustrations with Hong Kong and its educational system, and my romantic relationship.

Yes, my romantic relationship with the person who was later to become my husband. He was a Chinese graduate student I had met at the University of Minnesota who, by coincidence, came back to Hong Kong the same year as I did. His name was Wilbert Wang Chun Lai, and his major was Business Administration. Just like my brother, he was three years older than me, was a bit taller and had many pimples on his face. I was attracted to him because of my loneliness. Or perhaps, because he was Chinese. Or perhaps I thought that he, as a fellow foreign student in Minnesota, would be able to share the same experience that I did. But I was wrong. We shared few common interests besides going to restaurants and seeing movies.

It was April 1973. I had to cram for the final examination of my Education course. I also had a fight with Wilbert over some very minor issues. I couldn't sleep for a few days. I spoke to Bob Lord. On his advice, I went to the doctor at the University's Health Centre. The doctor there gave me some pills to take, after which I could sleep very well and was able to concentrate on my studies once again.

I told my mother about the pills. At once, she snatched the pills away from me, forbidding me to take them.

"Why shouldn't I take them?" I yelled to her in a combination of Chinese and English.

"You simply shouldn't. They are harmful to you," she said and confiscated my pills.

With the tension of my encounter with my mother, my fight with Wilbert, and my worries about not passing the exam, I lost more sleep.

I left the apartment to show my defiance. A mutiny, I thought. Yet without much money, I eventually had to call my brother up. He took me back to the apartment. My behaviour must have appalled and wor-

ried my mother. She had always thought that I was an obedient daughter. An obedient Chinese daughter should always listen to her elders.

She also must have thought that I was insane. Such behaviour was unacceptable and inappropriate. With my father away in Bangkok for his business trip, my mother immediately asked my godmother, a nurse herself, to have a psychiatrist to come to see me in the apartment.

Before the psychiatrist arrived, I was forced to lie on the bed of my parents' bedroom with my mother, my godmother, and my Amah Hing standing over me. My Amah Hing had to give me a basin bath, with me naked in front of the three of them.

"Let me out, let me out! All I want is sleep! I'll be alright!" I yelled in English, a language in which I could express myself much better than Chinese in times of crisis.

Not understanding English, they must have thought that I was more insane than ever. The psychiatrist, Dr. Chiu-Lung Wong, came to see me after talking to my mother outside the room. Like a typical Chinese businessman, he wore a tie and a suit.

"How do you feel, Ms. Kwok?" He asked me in his accented English.

"Let me out of this room! I need to sleep. That's all! I'm not a mental case! I don't have to see a psychiatrist!"

"It's OK, Ms. Kwok. But I'll give you a shot first."

"What is it that you're going to give me? I won't take it!" I cried in desperation. In the States, doctors always tell patients the nature of the medications they prescribe. Why couldn't this psychiatrist? I felt I had the right to know.

Yet I was not allowed to rebel. Like Christ about to be crucified, Amah Hing, my mother, and my godmother held me tightly and in came the shot. The psychiatrist left. Eventually, I was tamed. I became quiet. After a while, I became more agitated than ever. I crawled down from the bed, protesting and yelling in English again.

My behaviour must have frightened my mother. Not knowing much about medicine, she probably must have felt helpless, bewildered. To see her beloved daughter in such a desolate state? With whom should she consult? She called the psychiatrist up. An arrangement was made for me to be hospitalized in the psychiatric ward of one of the nicest, private hospitals in Hong Kong. At the insistence of my mother, my second uncle had to drive me to Central Hospital in my pajamas, crying like an unwilling Chinese bride forced to take part in an arranged marriage in the olden days.

I stayed in the psychiatric ward of the hospital for two weeks. I had a private room with a private bath. The hallway was dark and unpleasant. I was not allowed to leave the room. As well as the nurses in the ward, I was watched around the clock by private nurses my mother had hired. Everyday, Amah Hing would take off my clothes and give me a bath. I had wanted to call my friends up, but instantly, the phone line was cut. My constant visitors were my mother, Amah Hing, Wilbert and, to my surprise, my half sister, Philomena. My half sister, twenty years older than I, had married when I was about four. My brother Bill and his girlfriend, Amy, visited me couple of times. The only other visitor was my high school teacher, Ms. Margaret Moore. My high school friends, the confidantes of my secrets, were all told by my mother not to visit me. Mental illness was a taboo and should be kept within the family.

Like a bird in a cage, I had to submit to the orders of Dr. Wong and the nurses. I hated this kind of barbaric, solitary confinement. Based on what did Dr. Wong commit me to the hospital? I hardly knew him and he had only talked to me for less than ten minutes. He never gave me a diagnosis, nor did he give me the names of the medications he was prescribing. Did he think that he was God?

All I knew was that the quickest ticket for me to get out of the hospital was to forsake the individualist values of America, the land of freedom and liberty, and to re-learn the Chinese value of familial obedience and conformity.

There was a window in the room, facing the street. Everyday, I would

stand by the window, watching the active world outside. Tears would come to my face. These were not tears of depression, but tears that I had for those oppressed souls who, like myself, were kept against their will, in worlds they had not chosen.

"What are you thinking now, Yeng?" Asked my mother, as she was wiping the dishes with the paper towels.

"Nothing."

"Really? What is it? Tell me."

"I'm just thinking of my hospitalization in 1973 in Hong Kong."

"What about it? It is all water under the bridge now. Why do you have to think about it?" Said my mother with disapproval.

"Tell me, why is it that after my discharge, you went to see Dr. Wong yourself instead of me but I was the one who had to take the medications?"

My mother was surprised that I asked. Pausing for a little while, she said, "see, I was afraid that you might get more disturbed if you had to be in a psychiatrist's office. It was for your own good. I was only concerned."

"Did he prescribe any medications for you?"

"No, of course not," bluntly she replied. "See, I was not sick. I was healthy. You were sick."

Was she afraid to admit that she had to see the psychiatrist too? Or did she really go to see Dr. Wong in my place? What medications did I have? Why was I kept in the dark?

"Maybe you should go home and rest now. Mom, you're tired."

"Are you sure that you will be OK?"

"I'm sure. Don't worry."

She packed the leftovers into her bag, gave me a smile, and touched me with her hands. She greeted the nurses at the station with her broken English and then she left.

I was left alone in 9 South again. Perhaps my hospitalization in Hong Kong was the result of my difficulties in cultural re-adaptation to Hong Kong? Or I was a victim of cultural clashes and misunderstandings? Or I was unable to learn the coping skills I needed in my relationship with Wilbert? Or was it my mother's over-concern and her panicky reaction to my changed behaviour? Whatever it was, I knew that my mother loved me very much.

Yes, if I had a voice, I would tell all the nurses and the doctors in the ward and everyone else in the world that, in spite of what had happened, I loved my mother very much.

Yes, if I had had a voice in Hong Kong back then, I could have changed the circumstances. I could have fought back against my involuntary confinement in the psychiatric ward. Yet I couldn't. By the same token, if I had a voice now in Canada, I could have made the psychiatrists and nurses understand me as a woman brought up in the Chinese culture in the colonial British days of Hong Kong who had adopted parts of the American culture. Yet I couldn't.

I was only a voiceless hostage, aimlessly spending each day in a first class Canadian prison, with no goals to look forward to, and with no date of release in sight.

Dear God,
When will my voice be heard?
Tell me, please.

Chapter twelve

MEMORY

My mother had just arrived at the ward. As always, she brought some delicious food from Chinatown.

"What's that, Mom?"

"It's roast pork. You know why I bought it today?"

"Why?"

"What date is it in the Chinese Lunar Calendar?"

I did not know. There was no calendar in the ward. Even if I had a calendar, I would not have paid any notice to the Chinese Lunar Calendar, except for Chinese New Year.

"Today is your father's birthday. Remember yesterday was the Mid-Autumn Festival? And your father's birthday is the day after the festival.

My Father Woon Lum

My Mother Shiu Ching

That's why I've got some roast pork to celebrate with you. He always liked to eat roast pork," said my mother. She smiled contentedly. "I also got you some moon cakes that I had last night with your brother. Come, let me open them for you. Go and get a plate from the lounge and we'll eat."

Oh, yes, my father's birthday. He was born in 1912. How could I

forget? Last night there was a full moon, shining brightly in the sky. Indeed, yesterday was the traditional Chinese Mid-Autumn Festival, a time to remember the rebellion of the Sung Dynasty against the Mongolians who were ruling the Yuan Dynasty. The rebels hid their messages of attack in the moon cakes and distributed them to others. Eventually, they succeeded in their uprising.

My father was devoted to his work. A typical workaholic. Even on weekends, he would still have to mind the factories of Dairy Farm. He would take us for a quick lunch in the New Territories, after which he had to supervise the factories, leaving us all waiting for him. As a child, I was bored. I never liked those trips.

He was intelligent and determined. Before he joined Dairy Farm as the Chinese Chief Engineer, he was working with the Wing On Company, a big department store. He was promoted to foreman after he had fixed the electricity problem when none of his seniors could. He did not have a formal education in English. Yet he had learned it on his own and was able to communicate with his non-Chinese bosses at Dairy Farm. Having been a chain smoker, he quit smoking immediately at his doctor's advice.

By the time I was in high school, my father had already left Dairy Farm and started an air-conditioning firm on his own. He had to go on business trips to Japan, Thailand, and Indonesia. When I was in Grade Ten, he was in Thailand for the whole year. Every time he returned from his trips, he would bring me back many souvenirs—Japanese dolls, Thai papayas, and Indonesian dried shrimps. When he was not on his business trips, if he was not busy, he would give me a ride home from school. In the car, we would joke and laugh. He was, on the whole, a fun-loving man.

Just like with my mother, there was little touching between my father and me. Perhaps it was a Chinese tradition for parents of my time. When I was sixteen, one day, my father wanted to hold my hand. Immediately I slid away from him.

"Dad, I'm a big girl now. You can't hold my hand anymore."

Aside from being our parents, my parents did not seem to have many interests or tastes in common. My father was a fun-loving man who liked jokes, but my mother seldom shared his jokes. My father was impulsive and emotional whereas my mother was subdued and calm. The only common activity that they shared was going to the Baptist Church every Sunday morning. But oftentimes, they would arrive late for the service. It was quite embarrassing for the whole family to walk into the church when the service was half over. They did share one common trait. They were generous to their friends and relatives. They would accommodate the children of friends who needed a place to stay and they were generous in giving money to relatives who were in need.

Yes, every year, before our immigration to Canada, my father would celebrate his birthday by having a big banquet for his friends. That was one of the few days that I looked forward to when I was little. At the banquet, there was a delicious nine-course meal with my favorite shark fin soup. My father would give me lai-see, a red envelope with money, when I bowed to him and poured him a cup of tea to show respect.

My father used to be quite skinny when I was about four or five. Everyday, he would take the tram with my Amah Hing and me to my kindergarten, St. Paul's Convent School, which was close to his firm, Dairy Farm, in Causeway Bay. He would buy me candies if I behaved. He was temperamental and, like most men, quite chauvinistic. When he was angry, both my brother and I did not dare to utter a word. When I was in Grade Six, we had to go through a Public Examination before we could go to Grade Seven. Only about eight thousand passed the examination and only six thousand would have their names published in the newspaper. My name was not published.

When my father heard the news, he became extremely angry with me. He became hysterical and chased me all the way from the living room to the bedroom with a big stick, shouting:

"You've such a good opportunity to study. Why didn't you do a good job? Look at me. I did not have much education, had to learn everything on my own. It's a tough world out there, my daughter. If you're stupid, then study more. If the bright ones can get a concept by reading it once, you can get the same concept if you study twenty times as much. Your failure is a loss of face to our family and me."

I cried and screamed in horror. When I was in high school, I lived in fear, worrying about beatings such as these if I did not do well at school. Yet I had also learned to work hard in school, burying my head in books, where I found a lot of consolation and satisfaction.

"What are you thinking, Yeng?" Asked my mother.

"About father."

"What about him?"

"About his virtues and his vices," I said jokingly to my mother.

"I know what his vices were. He never drank or gambled, but…"

My mother did not continue, but gave me a smile—a smile that I understood pertained to her relationship with my father.

"Come, let's eat the moon cake and the roast pork." My mother changed the subject.

The moon cake is a moon-shaped cake, made with red bean and lotus seed fillings, that sometimes has a yellow egg yolk to it. It has the meaning of "tuan yuan"—reunion among family members.

As I was eating my moon cake with my mother, I thought of December 17, 1984.

It was a cold winter night. The wind was strong and it was snowing. It was one in the morning. My mother and I were walking slowly from Mount Sinai Hospital to our apartment at One Park Lane, which was close by the hospital on University Avenue and Dundas Street. The doctor had just informed us that my father had died of a massive heart attack.

How could it have happened? And so quickly? I did not cry. I could not cry. I was shocked. Only four days before, he and I had gone to the

Citizenship Branch on St. Clair Avenue. He was healthy, joking about his chubbiness. Only two hours before he was eating his dinner at home. He complained of chest pain, fell in the bathroom, and fainted. My mother became panicky. I called 911. The paramedics, the firemen, and the police came. Within seconds, they took him to the emergency room of Mount Sinai Hospital. That was it. The last time I saw my father alive.

Love and hate blended into oneness through death. In this windy night, they had become part of the past. My father would be silent forever.

Friends and relatives flocked to the funeral home, trying to offer words of comfort. Yet they were no use. The pain of loss and the acceptance of his sudden death, I cannot describe.

At York Cemetery, slowly my father's coffin descended into the grave. As the pastor said the prayer, I began to doubt the eternity of man. We are all vulnerable and transient. And we all have to go through the inevitable passages of life—birth, aging, sickness, and death. There is no escape. Life is like a lonely ship, sailing on its sea passages to a nowhere land.

We visited the grave about two months later. A tombstone had already been erected. It was still very cold and windy. I stood by the grave. All at once, I felt a sense of loneliness. Perhaps it was my fear of life and death? Yet at that moment, life and death were all tangled in this moment of silence and timelessness. I felt somehow that my father was still alive, that he was still part of me.

"Mom, do you know that father has been dead for about fourteen years now?"

"I know. Time really flies, right? My turn will be coming soon."

"Don't say it."

She looked at me. "It's a fact of life. Just make sure that you take your medications and look after yourself. That's my only worry."

"Today is the next day of the Mid-Autumn Festival. We are supposed to be joyful and be happy that we are together. You had dinner with brother Bill yesterday, right? How did it go?"

"Fine. The usual. We had dinner at this Chinese restaurant with him and his family. His daughter, Jenny, is doing well these days. She is pretty too. I even talked long-distance with his son, Edmund, in Hong Kong. It was nice to hear his voice. Oh, by the way, your sister Philomena called from California too. She wished me well. And she said hello to you too. She hopes that you will get out of the hospital soon."

"Say thank you to her for me when you call her."

Edmund, Jenny, me, sister Philomena. sister-in-law Amy, brother Bill

"Yeng, when can you get out of this place? You seem to be doing quite well these days."

"I don't know. I hardly see Dr. Yiu, except for some very brief visits."

"Once you get out, we'll go to your father's grave with your brother. I'm sure that your father will be happy in heaven to see us go there."

"Certainly, Mom."

Another inmate, Andrea, came to the dining lounge. She smelled the delicious food.

"What is it, Caroline?"

"Roast pork and moon cakes. Want to try some?"

"Sure. When I was in Jamaica, the Chinese there also celebrated the

Mid-Autumn Festival. By the way, I'm one quarter Chinese. My great-grandmother was Chinese."

Two more inmates, James and Sophia, joined in. Then, the two nurses, Natalie and Pat, came.

"What's up? Who brings the goodies?" Asked Nurse Natalie.

"My mother, of course," proudly I said.

"Gee, you're spoiled. Every day, your mother comes with delicious Chinese food. The other day, it was lobster, and today, it is roast pork," said Nurse Pat.

"Eat," said my mother, pointing to the moon cakes and the roast pork. "Today, my husband's birthday."

"OK, I'll just have a bite," said Nurse Natalie. "Oh, the roast pork really tastes good. Thank you, Mrs. Kwok."

My mother was happy while she watched them eat. Perhaps she was thinking of the days when she sat every morning watching my father eat his breakfast. I started humming the song, *Memory,* to myself:

"Daylight, I must wait for the sunrise,

I must think of a new life,

And I mustn't give in.

When the dawn comes

Tonight will be a memory too,

And a new day will begin…"

Yes, memory of my father on his birthday. And in a few years from now, there will also be memory of this impromptu party in the Concentration Camp of 9 South where both patients and nurses joined in.

Dear father, Happy Birthday.

Dear God,
Thank you for
The memory of my father.

Chapter thirteen

The Parole

"You can have a pass for this weekend, Caroline," said Dr. Yiu. How delighted I was to hear this news! Like a political prisoner who had received her amnesty, I jumped with joy upon hearing this pardon.

"But you have to wait until someone comes to pick you up."

"Why?" I asked, like a timid mouse, without raising my voice. An assertion of any kind might have ruined my chance for parole.

"Because I'm afraid that you may not be able to cope with life outside of the ward. After all, you've been here for over two and a half months."

I did not agree with her. But I did not voice my opinion. She must have assumed that I was an invalid, labeled as a "manic depressive". Yet had I not traveled on my own all over the States and Europe? I wondered if she had done the same herself. Why should I be afraid of the outside world? I belonged to the world outside, not this ward!

Happily, I phoned my mother and told her of the good news.

"Are you sure that you can go out for the weekend? Is this what Dr. Yiu told you?"

"Yes, Mom. You can speak to Dr. Yiu if you don't believe me."

"Why do they have to let you go out for the weekend?"

"To adjust me back to the reality of life outside. Come and pick me up, please."

I hung up the phone. Even my mother did not seem to trust me. Being locked up in a psychiatric ward had probably made me lose my credibility forever. People must think that I was simply a nut without any sound judgment at all.

Quickly I took off the hospital gown and changed back to my dress. I hated that hospital gown! It was so plain and ugly. I sat on the chair opposite the glass window of the nursing station. Inside, I was anxious and excited. But I had to hide my feelings. Too much excitement or

anxiety might lead the nurses think that I was still "manic" and should not go out.

I overheard the conversation between Nurse Pat and Nurse Gloria.

"Caroline has been in the ward for such a long time. Her behaviour is quite cooperative and she is pretty pleasant. I was just wondering why it is that Dr. Yiu does not discharge her," said Nurse Pat.

"I heard that it has to do with the lack of social support that she has outside the hospital. Her mother does not speak English. Perhaps Dr. Yiu is afraid that she might relapse. She was hospitalized in the ward in the early nineties."

"That's too bad. 'Cause I honestly think that Caroline could survive much better if she were not kept as an in-patient here."

"I think so too," said Nurse Gloria. "But what can we say? We're only nurses. It's the doctor who makes the final decision."

"But we know our patients better than the doctor. The doctor only comes to see them very briefly and infrequently."

"Well, go and study for a degree in psychiatry. Then, you'll be able to make decisions," teased Nurse Gloria.

Nurse Pat laughed.

"Actually, I quite like Caroline. She is funny and quite lively too."

"Yes. But when she first came in, I didn't know her. Her constant crying really was something. If there is someone for her to talk to and to calm her down, she becomes fine again," said Nurse Pat.

"I find the same thing about her too. She always seems to speak fast. That's what her mother told us. But don't forget that Cantonese is a fast language. So when she was distressed and had to speak English, her speech sounded like pressured speech to the psychiatrists. That's a symptom of being in a manic state."

"Yes, perhaps. And she seems hyper too. Maybe it is in her blood."

"Maybe. Anyway, let's get back to work now," said Nurse Gloria.

They did not know that I had eavesdropped on their conversation.

Indeed, they were right. Seeing me as an Asian immigrant patient, my crying must have scared those psychiatrists and nurses off. Perhaps they thought that Asian women were always reserved in their expression of feelings. And of course, I must have rambled on with my English that sounded accented and jerky when I was in desolation.

A while later, my mother came. I signed my name in the "out" book and left.

When I got out of the hospital, I felt like a captive freed from hostage. This feeling of joy and freedom was beyond description. I looked at the people on the street. Had I not always wanted to be among this crowd too? Here I was. My dream had come true.

We took the subway and got off at the St. Clair Subway Station. To walk on Yonge Street again was exciting and to see all the familiar shops there, Tim Hortons, St. Clair Market, Shoppers Drug Mart, Roots, and Second Cup, was a plus.

There was a lot of mail when I got into my apartment. One piece of mail was from my girlfriend in Hong Kong; it was a Hymn book from my high school. In the book, she wrote: *To my good old friend, Fei-Yeng: Best, Chee Man."*

I was moved. All at once, I thought of the traveling that I did with her in the eighties. We went to London, Paris, Amsterdam, Barcelona, Heidelberg, Frankfurt, and Lisbon. I hadn't seen her for about eight years now.

I called her up. She was surprised that I was in the hospital, but was glad that I was now on parole. We joked about old times, talked about our travels, laughed at our secrets, and sang our favorite hymn, *Stand Up, Stand Up For Jesus.* I sang my own version of the song to her:

"Stand up, stand up for yourself,
And never be afraid.

I know that I can make it,
Until the very end."

"Wow! You mean you're making lyrics these days? I never knew that. Yes, you should stand up for yourself and not be afraid in your fight against your illness. I'm sure that you will win one day and rise above those who have looked down on you. But first, be strong and forget about Phillip. Why don't you get well first then come to Hong Kong for a visit? You'll love Hong Kong and you'll see all our girlfriends here, OK?"

"Sure, I will."

To hear her voice was a consolation. Now that I was at home, I was able to make phone calls without restraint. I was so relieved to be able to connect with my friend. In the ward, I had to have twenty-five cents for each call. And of course, no long distance calls.

There was food in the refrigerator.

"Who bought the food? The fridge was empty when I left."

"Of course, it's me," said my mother. "Who else? I have your key, remember?"

I was touched. After all, mother is the best. Motherly love is unconditional.

"Why don't you stay with me for the weekend, Mom?"

"You're sure that you want me to?"

"Sure."

I went to my bedroom to make the bed for my mother. There on the end table was the picture that Phillip and I took last year. I looked at it. Slowly I put it back into my drawer where I kept all my junk. That was it.

That night, my mother and I had stir-fried fish and tofu soup. We sat down and watched a Chinese video together. For the first time in many years, my mother and I seemed to be connected once again. Except for her occasional reminder of my taking of the medications, there was peace and harmony between us once again.

The next day, I went up to Pacific Mall with my mother in Scarborough. Built in the early nineties, this mall is a modern Chinese mall that resembles some of the shops in Hong Kong. Shopping in their boutiques, I felt as if I were back to Hong Kong. We had dim sum in the restaurant there. Then, I had my favorite mango bubble tea. We also bought some groceries before we went home.

I slept very well for the two nights out, dreaming of Hong Kong and my friends who lived there.

Sunday evening was time to return back to my captivity, the hospital. I took a last peep at my apartment before I left. From the bottom of my heart, I wished that I could have a complete release soon.

When I returned to the ward, Nurse Gloria greeted me.

"How was your pass, Caroline?"

"Fantastic. You wouldn't believe." I started to tell her about my parole activities.

"That's wonderful. Now, change back to your hospital gown. And I'll give you the medications in a short while."

I looked at my mother. She gave me the candies that we bought at the mall. Then she nodded and smiled.

"There you go, Caroline. Listen to the nurse. I'll come by tomorrow to see you."

She left. Outside, it was dark already. Would my mother lose her way? No, she wouldn't. I saw the stars and a full moon in the sky above. Yes, the stars and the moon would guide her back to her apartment, safe and sound.

Dear God,
Thank you for
Giving me my parole.

Chapter fourteen

The Prisoners Of War

Once again, I was locked up in the single room with a security guard barring me. Yet had it not been just a few days ago that I was well enough to have the weekend pass and to leave the hospital? Or was it because of the excitement that I had on my days out that had caused me to be isolated again? No, not at all.

It was July 1, Canada Day. But this year, 1997, Canada Day had a special meaning to me. It was on this day when Hong Kong was no longer a British colony and became a part of China. As an overseas Chinese, I was extremely delighted at this historical changeover.

There was a documentary on the CBC Channel that evening about the changeover. It was at eight o'clock shortly after dinner. In the lounge, Jen and I were glued to the television. There were four other patients there. One was Edward, an Anglo Canadian, who suffered from personality disorder. He was right in front of the set. James, a young Jewish doctor, who had depression, sat quietly at the far end of the lounge. Sophia, a woman in her early thirties who suffered from post-partum depression, sat next to James. And Andrea, a woman from Jamaica, sat next to Jen and me.

She had been diagnosed as a schizophrenic.

"Everyone, this is Hong Kong! Look at all the high rises and the new Convention Centre!" Excitedly I said as I pointed at the pictures on the screen. "Look, here is Jiang Zemin, the Premier of China, shaking hands with Prince Charles. The Flag of the People's Republic of China is hoisting up now! Hurrah! Hong Kong is no longer a British colony!"

Yes, I was glad of this historical event in Hong Kong. The colonial days of Hong Kong stayed very well in my mind. I had to study English in an English-medium school with all my teachers, except for those in

Chinese and Chinese Literature, non-Chinese. Our examination system was modeled after the British system. The Governor and the Chief Executive Officers were always Caucasians from Britain while over ninety-nine percent of the population was Chinese. Their houses were always spacious in those upscale parts of Hong Kong. Never had I seen any non-Chinese living in resettlement buildings. At one time, when Princess Alexandra and her husband visited Hong Kong from England, I had to line up on Garden Road with my other classmates, waving a British flag.

As a little girl, I often wondered why Chinese could not rule Hong Kong. The answer from my teachers and my parents was that Hong Kong had become a British Colony shortly after the Opium War in 1841.

As I listened to the National Anthem of China and saw the children waving the flags of the People's Republic of China, I could not restrain from joy.

"Jen, turn the volume up a bit. Listen to the National Anthem!"

"Come off it! I had enough!" Edward yelled loudly.

Jen hesitated and looked at me.

"Go, Jen. Don't be afraid. He doesn't own the television," I said.

Jen was about to turn the volume up when Edward snapped at us again.

"You know something, girls? This is Canada. We should be watching some news about Canada."

"But Edward, this is once in a lifetime. Don't forget that most of the time, you are the one who monopolizes the television," I raised my voice.

"I don't care. Turn off the television," commanded Edward. He stood up and was about to change the channel.

"Why should I? It is about Hong Kong. I was born there."

"So what? You're now in Canada."

I did not pay any attention to him. He sat down again.

"Do the rest of you mind?" I asked the other prisoners in the lounge.

James and Sophia both shook their heads and said no.

"It doesn't bother me," Andrea said. "I know how you feel. I remember that I was exuberant when Jamaica became independent from the British in 1962."

"See, there you are, Edward. The majority wins!" I said, ignoring him. We continued to watch the documentary. Edward sat there, feeling defeated. He took a pillow and covered his ears.

"Listen to the National Anthem of the People's Republic of China! It is so impressive. When I was little, I had to sing *God Save the Queen*," I said.

"Yes, we had to sing the same Anthem too," said Andrea.

"Hey, Andrea, do you want to listen to us sing the National Anthem of China?" I asked.

"Of course, I don't mind."

"OK, let's go. Jen, why don't you lead because you can speak Mandarin better than me."

> *"Arise, ye who refuse to be slaves!*
> *With our flesh and blood,*
> *let us build our new Great Wall!*
> *The Chinese nation faces its greatest danger,*
> *From each one the urgent call for action comes forth.*
> *Arise! Arise! Arise!..."*

Jen started singing and I joined in.

"Come off it, for God's sake! I can't understand a word!" Edward shouted again.

We lowered our voice a bit, but continued to sing.

> *"Millions with but one heart,*
> *Braving the enemy's fire.*
> *March on!*

Braving the enemy's fire,
March, March! March on! March on! On!"

"I like your singing," said Andrea. "Don't you agree, Sophia?"

"Yes."

"How about you, James?"

James did not reply, but his eyes showed that he also agreed.

"You know something? The other night, I made up a song about Hong Kong," I said. "Want to listen?"

"Sure, why not?" said both Jen and Andrea.

Proudly I stood up as if I were my American folk singer idol, Joan Baez. After all, I was in a folk song group in high school. All the happy moments of my childhood days flooded my memory.

"God bless my Hong Kong,
Where I was born,
Just to say good-bye.
In July this year,
No more trumpets, my dear,
Oh what will happen to my land,
That I so love and hate?
Will I be able
To see the Harbour
And the Peak again?
In Canada, I can't be with you,
Be harmony and dignity,
Forever with you,
Be harmony and dignity,
Forever with you."

"Bravo, Caroline! I can't believe it. You used the melody of *God Save the Queen,*"

Andrea exclaimed excitedly, laughing.

Everyone enjoyed the song and applauded, except Edward.

"I've had enough of your songs, Caroline. An insult to the Queen!" Edward shouted.

Instantly he rushed out of the room.

"Well, probably he goes to the smoking room again," said Andrea.

"Yes, probably. He is a chain smoker," I said.

"And an alcoholic too," said Jen.

"Worst of all is that he likes to pick on others," said Andrea.

At that moment, Nurse Cheryl, a Caucasian of about thirty, came into the lounge. Unlike some other nurses, she had always been unfriendly and hardly smiled.

"What's going on? Why are you guys so noisy?" She said in her usual punitive voice.

"We were watching the documentary on the changeover of Hong Kong to China. That's all," I replied.

"But I heard you sing too."

"Yes, I sang. Do you want to listen to it again?" I was about to start singing.

"No, your singing disturbs others."

"Disturbs who? You all love the song, don't you?" I raised my voice, as I looked around for support from the other prisoners of war.

"We love the song. You should have listened to it too!" said Jen and Andrea. Even Sophia nodded her head and James smiled.

"But how about Edward? He had to leave the lounge," said Nurse Cheryl.

"That's his problem," I said. "So what? He's always like that. How about him shouting at me and insulting me?" I became indignant.

"How did he insult you?"

"He told me to turn off the television when I was watching the documentary on Hong Kong. And he wanted me to shut up when I sang my version of *God Save the Queen.*"

"Your version of *God Save the Queen?*"

"Yes. I'm creative and make lyrics. Do you want to listen to it?"

"No, I don't. You should stop singing. You're disturbing him and the nurses too. We have to work, don't you know?"

"But this is the patients' lounge. Everyday, there aren't any activities for us to do here. We just sit around, doing nothing."

"We do have activities in the ward."

"Like what?"

"We have the meditation group and we have the pet program. But you never join any of them."

"'Cause I don't like them. Why can't we have some reading programs with daily newspapers or books? That would keep our minds occupied."

"Well, we don't want you to be too stressed."

"How about having a music night? See the big baby grand piano there? Whenever I tried to play the piano, I was told that it was too loud. Why is there a piano there in the first place? Just for show?" My voice had escalated to a high pitch.

"Caroline, calm down. You're making a mountain out of a molehill," said Nurse Cheryl in her condescending and calm manner. "Listen, don't sing that song again."

She left without looking at me. Jen came and patted on my shoulder. Like a prisoner of war who had to listen to and endure the tortures of her captors, I had to submit to the order of the nurse. I thought of the submissions of many Chinese in the past to the British. But today was a triumphant day for Hong Kong that marked the end of the colonial era. Why should I be afraid and be intimidated by Nurse Cheryl and Edward?

In defiance of Nurse Cheryl's order, I sang my version of *God Save the Queen* louder than ever. Let the nurses and the doctors know of my patriotism to Hong Kong. Let them think that I am a "manic."

"God bless my Hong Kong,
Where I was born,
Just to say good-bye…"

Just before I was about to finish singing the song, Nurse Cheryl came into the room again. This time, Dr. Wendy Yiu was with her.

"Come on, Caroline, listen to me. Don't sing, OK? You're getting too hyper," said Dr. Yiu.

"Why should I? You're Chinese too, aren't you? Aren't you proud that today, Hong Kong goes back to China?"

"Well, but your behaviour is inappropriate."

"What do you mean by inappropriate? To sing the National Anthem of my native land is inappropriate? I have feelings for my native land. Perhaps you don't. Or you're too Canadian," I challenged her.

"Nurse Cheryl, give her the medication."

"I won't take it. What is it? I have the right to know."

"It's haloperidol 10 mg., Caroline."

"It's an antipsychotic medication. *I won't take it!* Let me talk to Dr. Ruskin. He is a senior psychiatrist in this hospital."

"But I am your psychiatrist here. You're under my care. Haloperidol would just help to calm you down, Caroline."

I looked at Dr. Yiu. Was her putting me back to the chemical restraint part of her job, as her way of making me conform to the routine of the hospital? She had never explained to me professionally about her reasons for giving such medication to me. To calm my "inappropriate" behaviour, perhaps? Had she talked to me in a decent manner, I would probably have been more cooperative.

I then looked at the other prisoners of war. They were intimidated by the intrusion of the doctor and the nurse. Now, they did not dare utter a word. It would probably be their turn if they disobey the orders of the nurse and the doctor. Jen could only give me an encouraging look. Same as Andrea, James, and Sophia.

I simply had no choice. It was beyond my power to fight back against this oppressive treatment. I knew that I had to conform to the system.

I swallowed the medication from Nurse Cheryl in front of my captor, Dr. Yiu, and the other prisoners of war. Before long, I realized that, unwillingly, I was kept in my solitary confinement once again in a lone cell with no more hopes for further parole.

Dear God,
Release us from our prison,
Please.

Chapter fifteen

The Human Touch

It had been days since I was put in solitary confinement again. Instead of talking to the wall, I expressed my feelings by writing some of the Chinese sayings that I knew when I was little. Going back to my culture and my happy childhood days were my ways of coping with distress. Yet none of the nurses and the doctors understood what I had written.

"Caroline, you've got some visitors," said Nurse Marilyn. She disturbed my concentration. Who could they be? My mother, my brother, his wife, and their daughter had just left.

As I looked up, I saw Dr. Joseph Wong, his sister, Alice, and my friend, Catherine, standing by my room. How delighted I was to see them! Alice, a woman in her early fifties with dark, short hair, knew my mother and me. Catherine, about my age and with a cheerful smile, had been my friend since the eighties. I was surprised to see Dr. Wong. After all, he had an extremely tight schedule.

"There you are, Caroline. Here are some apples and some sautéed shrimps for you," said Dr. Wong. "We just had our lunch in Chinatown and thought that we might drop by to see you."

"Eat the shrimps while they are hot. I'll peel the apples for you," said Alice.

"What are you writing?" asked Catherine.

"Well, just some Chinese sayings."

"Show them to us."

Proudly I showed them what I had written. After all, it was nice to be understood, wasn't it?

"To dissolve one's anger and sorrow into strength, failure means success; and determination can lead to success."

"Good for you, Caroline. I never knew that you know these Chinese sayings," said Dr. Wong.

"Of course I do. Just like you, I am Chinese from Hong Kong. My mother and my uncle used to teach Chinese Literature to me. It's just that in Canada, I seem to have lost quite a lot of it. They are excellent mottos that keep me going when I am here," I said. "There's another poem from the Tang Dynasty that I've also written down from memory."

"Read it to us," said Dr. Wong.

"OK. Here it is:

> *'In front of the bed is moonlight,*
> *Just like the hails on the road.*
> *I look up at the bright moon.*
> *When I look down,*
> *I think of my homeland.'"*

"That's very good," said Dr. Wong and Catherine.

Yes, to think of my homeland in this moment of isolation and confinement was the best solace for me.

"You know how I picked up my Chinese again? From looking at the Chinese poems in your office."

"Oh, then, I'm happy about that."

"Can you tell the nurses about what I had written, Dr. Wong?"

"I'll try, but I don't know if they are going to listen to me, though. See, I don't belong to this hospital. I only visit you as a friend."

"That's fine. As long as you guys understand that I am not that insane."

"You're definitely not insane," said Dr. Wong. Catherine and Alice echoed.

Nurse Marilyn interrupted their visit.

"Caroline, you've got a letter from the States."

Immediately I opened the letter. I knew that the letter must come from Richard Selzer, a surgeon and a writer, who was my professor at Yale University. We had been writing to each other since I left Yale in 1996. He knew of my hospitalization.

"Well, we'd better get going and leave you alone. Take care. We'll come some other time," said Dr. Wong.

They left. I read the letter.

(Note: Some friends use my Chinese name, Fei Yeng)

"Dear Fei-Yeng:

I know that you are in the hospital. Don't worry too much. I'm sure that you will get better and be out soon. I was sick with Legionnaire Disease years ago and was in a coma for three weeks. But I survived and wrote a book about it. I'm sure that you can do the same and, perhaps, write about your hospitalization and your illness one day. I know that you can do it. Just concentrate on getting well right now. Write to me if you have the energy to. And let me know once you are out of the hospital. Am thinking of you.

With warmest wishes,

Richard

This letter certainly was a great comfort to me. His belief in me as a writer and his concern for me were the best medicine of all.

During my confinement, there were other visitors too. Two of them were Alex and Maria Arokiam. They were my former tenants from India. They visited me several times and brought me some freshly squeezed juices. The other visitors were my family friends, Henry and Shirley Ho. They came right to the hospital once they knew of my hospitalization. They even brought me six big bottles of water. Then, there was Donald, Catherine's husband, who, together with Catherine, listened to me patiently for hours.My friends from high school, Ken, Helena, and Joanna, also visited me. Though I hardly go to church, Reverend Wong visited me too.

There were Ken Ho and his wife who brought homemade dishes to me. There was William Po, another family friend. He had just graduated from the University of Toronto and was about to leave for Hong Kong.

Yet he spent hours listening patiently to my stories. Then, of course, my brother who bought me some delicious buns from the Chinese bakery, and his wife, Amy, who kept a daily log for me.

August 26 was my birthday. I had been in the hospital for over two months now. At my request, the nurses organized a birthday party for me. Angelina and Betty, colleagues from my school, and my mother were there. They jammed in my room with Chinese noodles and chickens that they bought from Chinatown. And of course, a birthday cake. There was lots of laughter and they all sang Happy Birthday to me.

After the party, I was left alone in my room once again. It was nice to have friends who showed their concerns for me. Yet perhaps, in their eyes, I was still an invalid with a mental illness. Out of the kindness of their heart, they would warn me of never having another relationship with men, that my involvement with men would make me sick again. Yet what they did not realize was that even for a person with an invisible disability as such, love to and concerns for others and from others are very important, perhaps even more so than those "normal" souls. We are, after all, human beings with basic instincts and needs. If they had more knowledge about what mental illness is, they would probably be able to give me more emotional support and understanding.

As I looked around at some of the other prisoners in the Concentration Camp here, I considered myself fortunate. Some of them never had any visitors. One woman, Susan, was from Orangeville, Ontario. She suffered from schizophrenia and had been in the hospital for over three months. Never had she received any visitors or any calls. Whenever she saw the delicious food that my mother brought for me, she would look at me with envy. I would share some of my food with her. And she ate it with delight.

Another man, Joel, was a loner. Everyday, he would isolate himself, gazing into a distance, as if in oblivion. He only activity was to smoke a few cigarettes in the smoking room after dinner. Was this self-imposed

isolation part of his illness? Or was he just lonely without any loved ones? But he would offer to make me tea whenever he saw me in the lounge.

Since I did not have the privilege to go down to the lobby, some of the comrades offered their help. Whenever Brad, a bearded man of about forty, went down to get a smoke outside, he would ask me if I would like some apple cider or orange juice. And of course, Tricia, a young woman with lovely blond hair, who, like myself, was diagnosed as a manic-depressive, went out of her way to buy body lotion for me from the Body Shop. Oh, there was also Nellie, an elderly lady with panic disorder, who sang *Red River Valley* with me in the dining room. And then there was John, a young professor with clinical depression, who smuggled some ice-cubes from another ward for my honey juice. There was, of course, Mary, a woman of about my age with depression, who gave me a pair of stone blue birds before her discharge. How thoughtful she was!

"I'll probably never see you again. Or even if we run into each other on the street, you probably won't recognize me. But I just want to give this pair of birds to you as a gift to say that I care about you, that we had shared our lives together in what others might call a nuthouse."

I was moved to tears as I hugged her. This moment of empathy and acceptance of each other's illness overwhelmed me. Did she imply that all the prisoners in the ward were blue birds kept in the cage? Or did she mean she herself, about to be free from the cage, has to challenge the world alone, like a freed bird, one more time? Again, I did not know. She did not tell me.

I must have to admit that in this Concentration Camp, there were some caring and understanding captors, though some appeared to be snobby and unfriendly. Yet who could blame them? Didn't they have to work long hours with different shifts? They were, just like us inmates, human beings with problems of their own too.

Nurse Natalie, a nurse from Quebec with a tomboyish look, came to my birthday party with a sugarless lollipop and candies, knowing that I am a diabetic. Nurse Gloria, a young nurse in her twenties, showed me her wedding pictures. And there was Nurse Pat, who was extremely patient with me. Some of the psychiatrists were nice too. Dr. Paula Ravitz, an American from Michigan, talked to me and contacted my friends for me. Somehow, probably because of my stay in Minnesota as a student, I could communicate with her very well. Besides, she was always cheerful with a smile. Dr. Krista Lemke, a young, lanky resident from Vancouver, was friendly and understanding. She sang *Puff the Magic Dragon* with me to help me pass through my lonely moments in the hospital. Dr. Ronald Ruskin was equally understanding. He read and responded to the poems that I had written in English.

These "human touches" really brightened up my days, adding some lively colours to my monotonous life in prison. They gave me hope that, in this world, there are some caring people, whether they are health care professionals, or friends, or inmates like me.

In my lonely cell, I made a secret promise to God that someday, when I got out of the hospital, I would try to help those so-called "nuts" or "nut doctors", to the best of my ability, within the limit of my skills, both as a professional and a survivor. I hope that the "nuts" will be able to communicate better with their doctors without fears or stigma and that the "nut doctors" will not intimidate their patients in their psychiatric treatments.

Hopefully then, mental institutions will become new havens of hope for many lost souls.

Dear God,
Grant me my prayer,
Please.

Chapter sixteen

THE HEARING

It was the middle of September. I had been in 9 South for about four months now. Since August, I had been given day passes and weekend passes. For my day passes, I would always go up to the library on the eighteenth floor of the hospital. I liked this quiet, intellectual environment. I would look at the different journals and books on surgery and psychiatry. It was there that I began to learn more about manic-depression, psychiatric treatments, and medications. Sometimes, I would just sit by the computer, pretending that I was one of the medical students. It reminded me so much of my days at the University of Minnesota.

Yes, I remembered Sarah Graffunder, my teaching assistant for the Modern Literature course at the time. She came to the Wilson Library at the university during a heavy snowstorm to give me extra help in writing my essay for the course. I would always be grateful for her generosity and encouragement as a foreign student. And of course, my other two professors, Shirley Garner and John Hurrell, whom I owe much gratitude for their inspirations.

Yes, I also remembered the many nights I spent in the library at the Ontario Institute for Studies in Education at the University of Toronto, doing research for my Master of Education course. And of course, I remembered the many conversations that Richard Selzer and I had in the Cross-Campus Library at Yale University.

Yet here I was kept as a captive, only allowed to be on parole, not knowing when the end of my imprisonment would be. This uncertainty of my release frustrated me more than ever. I had to get an OK order from my captor, Dr. Wendy Yiu. But she hardly had any individual sessions with me. Most of the time, I talked to the different nurses on duty. How could she understand me? How could she know of my progress?

I decided to type a letter on the computer, asking for release from this prison. The letter ended with a plea to the Members of Parliament for help if she still did not want to discharge me. I showed the letter to the nurses and Dr. Yiu.

"This is my letter, Dr. Yiu. I want to be out of this ward. If not, you wait and see. I will contact the Members of Parliament about this inhumane hostage taking," I threatened her for the first time, at the risk of being put back in isolation.

She was surprised. She looked at me through her black-framed glasses.

"I don't think that you're ready to be discharged yet. But if you insist, I'll see to it."

Not ready to be discharged? I did not understand. Had I not tried my best to behave after the isolation incident on July 1? I did not dare to make a sound in the ward afterwards. Like an obedient slave, I did not struggle against the nurses' orders.

Two days later, Nurse Marilyn told me of a pre-discharge meeting with Dr. Yiu, the social worker Lieve, and herself. My threat had really worked! In the meeting room next to the baby grand piano, the four of us sat together.

"Caroline, how do you feel now?" Asked Dr. Yiu.

"Fine."

"I mean your mood. Do you feel that you're stable enough? From zero to ten, how would you rate your mood?"

I paused for a moment, then guessed, "five." How could I rate my mood according to such a scale?

"Do you think that you are different from when you first admitted?"

"Yes, I think so."

"In what ways?"

"Well, I am calmer and less distressed," I answered. I had to give her this answer. After all, that was what she wanted to hear, wasn't it?

"Do you think that you can handle the outside world?"

"Sure, why not? Have I not shown you how well I coped when I had my weekend passes?"

"But you will be living on your own, though."

"Sure, I can manage," I said. I wanted to tell her that I had been living on my own since I was eighteen as a foreign student at university in the States, but I didn't. Why should I? She probably could not understand anyway.

"Do you know what medications you are taking?"

"Yes. I'm on epival and clonazapam."

"How often do you take them?"

"Three times a day, morning, noon, and evening."

"What do you want to do after your discharge?"

I hesitated. I really did not know. I knew that I could not go back to teaching until the school board's doctor had approved. Yet teaching had always been my life. Every morning, at a quarter to nine at the latest, I would open the door of my classroom for the students to get in. Then, right at nine, the National Anthem, *O Canada,* would be on the PA, followed by the announcements for the day. This routine had become my ritual.

"To learn to swim," I lied, not wanting to give them the impression that I did not have any goals after discharge.

I was told to leave the room for a minute. They had to discuss more about my discharge. Nervously I waited outside, as if I were a prisoner in a court, waiting for the sentence for my crime. What were they discussing? Would they retain me again? Or would they set me free? What would be the verdict?

They came and asked me to go in.

"I'm still a bit hesitant about discharging you, Caroline," said Dr. Yiu.

I wanted to cry and to scream at her. But I had to control myself. Don't ruin your chance, Caroline! Control your emotions. Talk slowly to her. Be rational.

"Why, may I ask?" I asked politely without raising my voice.

"Well, it's just that you have been here for about four months now. I'm afraid that you might have difficulty in taking care of yourself."

"But Dr. Yiu, if you don't believe me, why don't you come to my apartment and see how I manage myself? That would be fair, to you and to me. Don't you think?"

She looked at the social worker, Lieve.

"What do you think?"

"That's an excellent idea, Dr. Yiu," said Lieve. "Maybe tomorrow, we'll visit your apartment with you. Can you make it tomorrow afternoon, Dr. Yiu?"

Dr. Yiu looked at her calendar.

"Yes, tomorrow's fine with me. Tomorrow afternoon at two then. I'll wait for both you and Caroline at the front desk. We'll go there by taxi."

I called my mother that afternoon and asked her to tidy the apartment for me. I had to show them that my apartment was spotlessly clean, to show them that I could cope with life. That night, I had trouble sleeping. I was worried about the final verdict tomorrow, after the visit.

It was a little before two the next day. I was all dressed up, waiting for Lieve and Dr. Yiu. We took a taxi to my apartment. Not knowing that my mother had been in the apartment that morning, they were surprised that it was clean and organized. I poured them some Chinese tea. They looked around and saw my piano.

"How long have you been playing the piano?" Lieve asked.

"Since I was eight."

Dr. Yiu was amazed by the many books that I had on the shelves in my study. She looked at them.

"You're interested in Chinese Literature too, right?"

"Yes, of course. I am Chinese."

They seemed to be happy with what they saw.

"Who would do the cooking for you after you are discharged?"

"I would do it myself. When I was at the university, I worked in a restaurant."

"Is there anything in your refrigerator now?"

"Take a look if you want," I said. I opened the refrigerator and was surprised to find that there were lots of foods there—vegetables, chicken, milk, and juice. My mother must have brought them that morning.

The inspection of these captors was complete. They were satisfied. Then came the verdict.

"We can discharge you tomorrow, Caroline. But you still have to see me afterwards once a week," said Dr. Yiu. "I'll be your out-patient psychiatrist."

"When will I be able to return to teaching?" I asked, anxious at having to stay home with nothing to do.

"Not until I think that you're one hundred percent recovered. Besides, you will have to see the board's doctor before you can go back."

Still, rejoice! Hurrah! Finally, I was released. I was no longer a prisoner. At last, I was free! Forget about teaching now. Just enjoy your regained freedom for a while, Caroline. I started to hum my song, *Free As The Wind:*

"Butterfly was in the sun
Taught me all that I needed to see
For they sang, sang to my heart,
Oh look at me, look at me,
Free as the wind, free as the wind,
That is the way you should be."

Dear God,
Thank you for
Setting me free at last.

Chapter seventeen

New Haven Of Hope

I was released from the hospital by mid-September. As I stepped out, I savored my first breath of fresh air in many months. To see life in motion and to watch the pigeons eating the leftover breads on the sidewalk meant the regaining of my freedom. For once, I was liberated from my captors who kept me a hostage. This feeling of joy was overpowering to me.

Though I could function just like any other human being, I could not go back to my teaching job with the school board until the board doctor approved. The morning calls from my mother promptly woke me up at seven every day. Afterwards, I was left with little to look forward to. In short, my life at home was like living in a prison without bars. My schedule was as follows:

1. Brush my teeth, wash my face, and take my medications.
2. Read the newspaper.
3. Watch *Canada A. M.* on television.
4. Fool around with my singing.
5. Play the piano for a while.
6. Do my writing and reading.
7. Depart to see Dr. Yiu and sometimes Dr. Wong.
8. Go to Chinatown and have lunch.
9. Every Thursday, take piano lessons at the Royal Conservatory of Music.
10. Every Sunday, go to church with my mother.

Bravo! Ten! Perfect Score!

Indeed, my house had become a new haven of hope in its own right. Yet the monotonous routine of my existence was devastating to my mind. There was little communication with my friends, except for the occasional get-well phone calls. I felt both emotionally and socially isolated.

I simply had to reclaim my life.

To tell you the truth, this solitary confinement in my house was hard to swallow.

Everyday, through my window, just like Laura in the Glass Menagerie, I watched the parades go by. I couldn't stand this fruitless existence. Yet what could I do? Quit my job? Be my mother's baby girl again? No, not at all. It would have been too self-defeating. Rather, I paid my visits to the doctors as well as to my dentist, Dr. Michael Shelegy. I also learned to pamper myself a bit by buying some sugarless chocolate and herbal tea for my own enjoyment.

By coincidence again, the United States has a town called New Haven in Connecticut where Yale University is located. It was at Yale University where I took my Creative Writing course with Richard Selzer as my professor.

In mid-November, I visited Yale University again. I took the greyhound bus and traveled to New York City. As the bus passed through Buffalo and Albany, I thought of my first arrival in the States as a foreign student. I remembered how I roamed around San Francisco by myself with a map on the first day after my arrival. I was surprised to find that Chinatown did not quite look like Hong Kong, but rather an ancient village in China. I was also surprised to see hippies lying on the benches in Union Square. And seeing the big redwood trees in the Golden Gate Park next to the majestic Golden Gate Bridge was breathtaking. Then, of course, I remembered my first day when I arrived in Minneapolis. It was spring 1970. The weather was extremely cold. For the first time, I saw snow. I was amazed by the old, brick buildings on the campus of the University of Minnesota with the Mississippi River flowing by. It was at here I took many of my courses in English Literature, French, Speech, and Drama. It was on this campus where I had some professors who were friendly, encouraging, and stimulating. Without them, I would have been lost in this huge university. It was also on this campus where

I worked part-time as a cleaning lady, a clerk, a tour guide, a waitress, a factory worker, and an undergraduate teaching assistant.

I also thought of my many travels in those days. Yes, to Chicago, New York City, Washington, D.C., and Los Angeles. In Chicago, I experienced the racial differences and tensions in America; in New York City, I saw the majestic buildings in Manhattan and the slums in the Bronx and in Harlem; in Washington, D.C., I sensed the historical presence of Abraham Lincoln; and in Los Angeles, I felt the wonders of Disneyland and Hollywood.

Yes, those were the days when I was as free as a bird without worries. Now, I could only look back in nostalgia with a grin.

From the Port Authority Station in New York City, I walked to the Grand Central Station to take the train to New Haven. Yes, Track 27—the same old track as it was a year ago when I went there to study. All of a sudden, I felt as if I were a devoted pilgrim in her holy pilgrimage to Mecca. As I looked through the window of the train, I saw blank treetops without leaves—colorless, just like my present exile from the school board.

I enjoyed this kind of solitary travel very much. It was an escape from the doctors and nurses in the hospital. A restoration of my pride and independence. A refreshment of my sanity. An affirmation of my confidence. Better than taking the tons of tranquilizers that I had been forced to take.

The buildings at Yale University's Central Campus were mainly of Gothic style architecture. As the taxi took me to the Holiday Inn, it passed by the Hall of Graduate Studies on York Street. It was in this dormitory that I stayed last year. Opposite to it was the Law School building. And a bit further down the road was the Sterling Library with its steeple. It was connected by an under path to the Cross Campus Library. The taxi turned left onto Broadway when it reached Elm Street. On Broadway, there were a small cinema, the Yale University Bookstore,

and some restaurants.

Richard Selzer came to meet me at the hotel on Whalley Avenue with his aged old Volvo. He was about sixty-nine years old with a pair of brown spectacles on his big, blue eyes, but he looked young for his age. He was delighted to see me. We then went to the Cross-Campus Library where I had spent hours as a student. It was in this library that I often ran into him. In this library, we chatted for hours about writers and poets. He took me to the fourteenth floor of the Sterling Library to look for two translated copies of Chinese poems. It was then that I found out that he had an interest in Chinese Literature.

Shortly before I was admitted to Yale, Dr. Wong diagnosed me as having a hypothyroid problem, probably as a result of my years of lithium intake. I took about fifteen pills every day—a combination of my hypothyroid and my manic-depressive medications. My whole body became itchy then. I told my problem to Richard, who suggested that I should first call Dr. Wong and go to the Health Centre of the university afterwards. I hesitated, afraid that the doctors would lock me up in the psychiatric ward.

"Don't worry. Ask the doctor to contact me if it's necessary," said Richard.

When I told the doctor at the Health Centre about it, she said, "you're lucky that you have Richard Selzer as your professor. He's amazing!"

Only then did I know that he was an icon in the field, a well-respected professor with many prestigious awards in both medicine and creative writing.

It was in his office in this library where he offered to read my medical chart.

"Your office is still the same—as messy as ever with your stethoscope and books all over," I said jokingly. "So lucky that your mind is not."

He grinned.

We then went to the Elizabethan Club of the university. There was complete silence there. Yet unlike the silence in 9 South at Mount Sinai, the students here were studying. I found this academic atmosphere extremely refreshing. It was a change of environment for me from my hospital confinement. There was a colleague of his who was a professor specializing in the work of Chaucer. Immediately, I thought of my days as an English major in Minnesota. Had I not once studied Chaucer too? Yet what had happened to my study?

He took me to the vault of the Elizabethan Club.

"Only a few professors know the combination to the vault and I am one of them," proudly he said.

Yet after a few tries with the combination, the vault still remained locked.

"I hope that you haven't suffered from Alzheimer's," I teased.

Embarrassed, he looked at me, again with a grin. Eventually, he managed to open the vault. When we were in the vault, I picked up Shakespeare's *Macbeth* and read aloud:

"Tomorrow, and tomorrow, and tomorrow
Creeps in this petty pace from day to day,
To the last syllable of recorded time,
And all our yesterdays have lighted fools
The way to dusty death. Out, out, brief candle!
Life's but a walking shadow, a poor player
That struts and frets his hour upon the stage
And then is heard no more. It is a tale
Told by an idiot, full of sound and fury,
Signifying nothing."

He stood next to me and listened attentively. It was one of the most stimulating experiences that I had ever had—the best cure for my manic-depression.

We had dinner at the Great Wall, a little Chinese restaurant near the campus. It was not a fancy restaurant at all, but seemed to be one of the few authentic Chinese restaurants in New Haven. Over dinner, he told me about some parts of his life, that he was born in Troy, New York, that his father was a family practitioner, that he was in the Korean War as the medical staff, and that he had been in Hong Kong.

"You mean you were in Hong Kong in 1955?"

"Yes, I was. You were just a little girl then."

I was astonished.

He also asked me a question that took me by surprise.

"I think that you were lonely when you were at Yale, weren't you?"

"Yes, I was. Just a little bit," I answered, embarrassed. Yet he did not know that the loneliest moments of my life were not at Yale, but they were the times when there was no communication between my ex-husband and me. Of course, I did not tell him.

The next day, we went to Yale University's Art Gallery on Chapel Street. Again, the silence of the Gallery with its exhibitions and sculptures overwhelmed me. He led me to one of the sculptures.

"This is Father Juan. And I have written an article based on it."

"What is it about?"

"Well, you'll find out."

"Can you send me a copy please?"

"Sure. And I want you to keep it."

I looked at him in amazement. For years, I had tried to abandon my love of the arts and literature for fear of getting sick again. Yet here I was, standing in front of a doctor-turned-writer, telling me of his writings. He was sane as always. Perhaps it was his love of the arts that had maintained his sanity despite his pressure at work. I decided, at that moment, that when I returned to Toronto, I would involve myself more in the arts.

The next morning, it was time to leave New Haven. He came to the hotel to see me off with one of his books, *The Doctor Stories*, which he

Richard Selzer and me at Yale University

gave to me as a present.

In the book, he wrote "To my Colleague In Writing, Caroline Fei-Yeng."

I was flattered.

"To be your colleague in writing? Have I been promoted to a writer?" I asked him.

"Sure, you are a writer. You took my creative writing course, didn't you?"

"Yes, but I haven't written a book yet!"

"Certainly, you will. I believe in you. You can do it, Fei-Yeng. Remember what I wrote you in my letter when you were in the hospital? You can write a book based on your experiences in the hospital and your illness. Then, I am sure that a lot of people will benefit from reading it."

"But English is my second language. I will never be able to make it. Do you think that I will get a publisher?"

"Fei-Yeng, trust yourself. Make writing your dream to look forward to. That will give you a purpose in your exiled life from the school board. Remember, life is an open road. There is always light at the end of the

tunnel. Never give up your hope. Nothing ventured, nothing gained. Remember this, OK?"

I nodded my head in gratitude. His encouraging words had already given me a New Haven of Hope. Yes, to write about mental illness and mental health. To eradicate the social stigma and the fears attached to the illness. And to help the mentally ill be able to participate in and be accepted by mainstream society.

He waved good-bye to me and headed his way to the library with his brown leather briefcase. I wanted to utter a word of thanks, but it was already too late. He was already gone.

On my way back to Toronto, as I sat on the bus, I saw a flock of birds flying in the clear sky. Weren't they beautiful? I realized that I was not Laura in the Glass Menagerie, crippled with a handicap. But rather, I am is Caroline Fei-Yeng, a fighter--a soldier with a cause.

Dear God,
Thank you for my visit
To New Haven.

Chapter eighteen

WHAT'S IN A NAME?

"What's in a name?
That which we call a rose,
By any other name,
Would smell as sweet,
So Romeo would,
Were he not Romeo called.... "
From Shakespeare's *Romeo and Juliet*

"You should listen to your doctor and take the medications. Don't ever skip any of the dosages. I don't want you to be sick again."

"You should not overstress yourself. Take life easy."

"You should stay out of any relationship. See, you can't handle any emotional stress."

"Don't read any books at all. Don't write anything. Just watch some television."

"Don't ever think of traveling on your own."

This was the advice from some of my friends and relatives after my release from the hospital. I was still an "abnormal invalid" in their eyes. I did not talk back to them. After all, they probably meant well, or they feared another hospitalization that might cause them to worry.

Yet at the bottom of my heart, I felt that I would always be a "second class" citizen to them. After all, I had been confined to psychiatric wards many times; I had to take leave from my teaching job, and I was labeled a "manic-depressive" by the psychiatrists.

They, many of them workaholics, could not comprehend mental illness and the reason I had to be off work. What did the word "manic-depressive" mean to them? They probably did not know. They just knew that I was sick and had to be locked up as a psychiatric patient. Besides,

the negative attitude of the media towards mental illness probably frightened them. The newspapers often put on sensational headlines about the shootings or the homicides by the mentally ill. Movies also tend to portray the mentally ill as simply crazy or retarded.

I gained weight. Instead of wearing size seven, I had to wear size fourteen. My stomach protruded. I then became the laughing stock of my relatives. "You look as if you're pregnant! Do some exercises," my mother would remind me every once in a while. I felt ashamed. What had happened to my beautiful figure? My skin, especially my knuckles, was pigmented too. "You didn't wash your hands, did you?" Some of my friends would tease me. I also became extremely thirsty, having to drink water all the time, sometimes non-stop. "What's wrong with you? Can't you stop drinking?" said my brother. My hands shook with tremors. I was not myself. I became very self-conscious. I *hated* it.

To them, the only cure for illness was to take the medications. They didn't know that a positive understanding of and a holistic approach to the illness is equally important to my recovery.

At the time I was in the hospital, when I called some of my friends up, they did not return my calls. Did my calls disturb their peace of mind? They did not know that a mentally ill person needs emotional support and understanding the most during her crisis.

On various occasions, right to my face, some acquaintances called me a crazy woman, a stupid ass, a retard, a witch. To them, this name-calling was just a joke. A lousy joke, maybe. Yet it really hurt me. Could I cry in front of them for these insensitive remarks? No, I couldn't. If I did, they would think that I was still not well. They would probably report to the psychiatrists about me according to their interpretations of my behaviour. I would then be hospitalized again. After all, all of my medical records showed only comments from my relatives. There was no input from me, the patient. I had to put on a smiling front to protect myself—a self-defense mechanism. At the same time, I pitied their ignorance of and disrespect for another human being with a hereditary disease. How would they feel if they were in my shoes? Solitary confinement for four months. Reputation lost. Fear of losing my job. Could they have survived? I wondered. Don't forget that, just like them, I am also a human being with feelings and emotions, with all my rights and privileges.

In spite of their name-calling, I don't blame them for their ignorance. Had they had more exposure to the experience of mental illness, their fears would have subsided. The social stigma would have been diminished.

Even I was confused with all the psychiatric terms. How could I expect them to fully understand? Bipolar Disorder. Depression. Anxiety disorder. Schizophrenia. Obsessive-Compulsive Disorder. What do they mean? What is their equivalence in Chinese? And what are the symptoms? Then come the names of the different medications--Prozac, Zoloft, Lithium, Epival, Artane, Cogentin, Chlorpromazine, Perphanazine, and Clonazapam.

What are their functions? And their side effects? Little information was given to me at the hospital. Or if it was given, the explanation was so very fast that it was difficult for me to grasp it.

Even to this day, I still don't quite understand the medical phrases defining the symptoms of manic-depression, such as flights of ideas, mood swings, and pressured speech. On what basis did the psychiatrist define these notions? On her preconceived ideas of what my behaviour as a Chinese woman should be? Or did she look into my uniqueness as a woman of colour? Did the psychiatrist really understand my expressions of emotions that might be different from the North American norm?

A self-defense mechanism that I had was to comply with the wishes of some of my friends and relatives. Don't talk back, Caroline, be an obedient China Doll. Maintain the Chinese philosophy of harmony, then you will be fine. But it was against my nature not to express my opinions. What could I do? To be cooperative was the key word. Had I not learned about it in the hospital? In short, I had become a mute, submitting myself to their wishes.

Once every two weeks, I would go to the Pharmacy By the Grange

on Dundas Street to get my medications. Every week, I would go to see Dr. Yiu for consultations. Once in a while, I would see Dr. Wong for my blood level check-up.

Visits to the Pharmacy and the doctors did not improve my sense of self-esteem much. At every one of these visits, I was considered a patient who did not have the ability to regain confidence. I belonged to the "inferior" category. Had I not once done counselling to my students at the school board? I was the authority to my students. Yet now, I was under the authority of these doctors.

I was especially uptight and intimidated by Dr. Yiu. She was the psychiatrist who wrote down every one of my behaviours during my sessions with her in her notepad. What if her observations were negative? That could have led to another hospitalization.

I was afraid to tell her of my aspirations as a writer, a journalist, a researcher in the area of cross-cultural psychiatry, a lecturer, and my interest in learning French. Had I not once ended up locked up in a mental institution when I told a psychiatrist about these aspirations? Psychiatrists could interpret them as "grandiose ambitions", a typical symptom of the "manic" phase. Very often, I would hide my true feelings from her. Besides, she would not be able to understand my feelings. She was not my long-time girlfriend whom I grew up with in Hong Kong. Why should I confide my feelings in her?

What's in a name anyway? Just as in Shakespeare's *Romeo and Juliet,* Juliet said to Romeo: *"Tis but thy name that is my enemy."*

By the same token, I gradually realized that manic-depression is only a name—a medical jargon for people of a lesser mind to look down upon, and to fear. Yet do they know that many talented artists and great politicians are manic-depressives? Van Gogh, Beethoven, Winston Churchill, Abraham Lincoln, Charles Dickens, and Ernest Hemingway are just a few to mention. Without Van Gogh, would there be famous post-impressionist paintings for the world to admire these days? Without Beethoven, would the world be listening to *Für Elise* and *Moonlight*

Sonata? Without Winston Churchill, the World War II would probably not have ended. Without Abraham Lincoln, would the slaves be emancipated? And Dickens was considered to be a great British writer of the Nineteenth Century while Ernest Hemingway was one of the greatest American writers of the Twentieth Century.

In fact, before I had been diagnosed as a manic-depressive, I played pieces by Beethoven when I was in Hong Kong. And when I was studying English Literature at the university, I always admired well-known poets and writers. I read John Keats' *Ode to a Grecian Urn*, Tennessee Williams' *A Streetcar Named Desire,* Eugene O'Neill's *The Iceman Cometh,* and Virginia Woolf's *To the Lighthouse.* I did not know that these artists had, like me, a mental illness. I should be proud of this "label." I can rank myself with all these famous people. Am I not lucky?

What I don't understand is that people can accept and sympathize with a person who has cancer or diabetes, but *not* mental illness. Why is it people with physical illnesses can be so open while the mentally ill often have to hide? It is a terrible social stigma. Don't people realize that one of the world's most common illnesses in the 21st century is depression or manic-depression, affecting millions of people, from the very young to the elderly? This invisible disability is as potent as other visible disabilities. Can't people see that the maintenance of one's mental health is as important as one's physical health, that they both affect each other?

These people with a shallow view can use whatever name they want to call me, either straight to my face, or behind my back. They seldom bother me now. I have learned to swallow these harsh comments. Each and every comment makes me stronger and stronger. In short, I have learned to develop my inner strength and endurance. I am not Brecht's *Mother Courage.* Rather, I am *Caroline Fei-Yeng Kwok.*

Dear God,
Let there be more
Acceptance of me,
Please.

Chapter nineteen

Bon Voyage

By February, I still could not return to work. The luxury of staying at home with the disability pension had become a pain in the neck. Besides the doctors' appointments and my piano lessons, there was hardly anything to do at home. I tried my best to stay happy. Yet oftentimes, I wasn't. My routine of going to work every day was disrupted. Every morning, at around nine o'clock, I would imagine that I was at the school, singing the National Anthem of Canada. Had I also suffered from separation anxiety disorder on top of my manic-depression?

The weather was below zero, too cold to get around. I could not stroll along the park, neither could I walk in the shopping malls all day. And I could not have dim sum with my mother in Chinatown every day either. I felt as if I were the Israelites in exile. But where was my Moses? Who would bring me back to Israel, the land of Canaan?

Chinese New Year was in February that year. So Bon Voyage! To Hong Kong and Beijing! I bought a ticket for my mother to go with me to visit my aunt and my uncle in Hong Kong. They were all over eighty. How many more years did they have? Why not let them see each other and enjoy the moment of reunion while they were healthy? Besides, during my hospitalization, my mother went to the hospital to see me every day. Buying a ticket for her was just a small token of thanks. I could also see all my good old friends from high school. Why not?

On February 11, my mother and I departed by Cathay Pacific on a long flight of eighteen hours to Hong Kong—a city that I had not visited for over eight years. As the plane began its descent at the airport at around 6.30 in the morning, I peered out the window, amazed by the high rises and the mountains that surround the Victoria Harbour. A few tankers and ferries were crossing the harbour. Beyond the crimson skyline were white flocks of clouds floating by.

After immigration and baggage claim, we went to the exit door. Already, among the crowds, my uncle of eighty-two was standing at the gate, waving his hands to us. Aside from his wrinkles, he seemed to be as energetic as years ago. The taxi took us through the crowded streets all the way from Hong Hum in the Kowloon Peninsula, through the Cross-Harbour Tunnel, then up the hill to Tai Hang Drive where my uncle's apartment was.

The apartment was small by North American standards, but was quite adequate with about eight hundred square feet. There were three tiny bedrooms with a small living room, a kitchen, and a bathroom. It was clean, decorated with colorful curtains, with a refrigerator and two televisions in the living room.

My aunt opened the door. Dressed in a brown suit with her dyed hair and make-up, she did not look like she was eighty-one at all. When I greeted her, I could see the warmth in her eyes. She had already prepared a room for us. Wasn't it nice? At that moment, I could feel the love and the warmth of my blood relatives. I had to sternly hold back my tears of joy in our reunion. It is still not common for Chinese to hug each other, nor is it to express feelings too much. Though I wanted to hug my aunt and my uncle, I didn't.

"Yeng and sister-in-law, have some tea and biscuits," said my aunt as she poured the jasmine tea into our cups. "Sister-in-law, you seem to have lost some weight. Don't you eat?"

My mother did not answer, but looked at me. Perhaps she felt that it was my illness that had worried her, that she did not eat much. All at once, I felt guilty.

Yes, all these years, my illness and hospitalizations had given her a tremendous burden in her old age. Her mind must have been tormented.

Being a workaholic herself before her retirement, she could not understand why her daughter had to be away from her job. She was afraid that I might lose my job. She could not understand much about manic-depression, except that, to her and a lot of Chinese, it is a social disgrace,

a loss of face to the family, an illness that must be hidden. She could not understand my relationships with men either. How could I have a divorce? How come I was not like her, accepting an unhappy marriage without any complaints? How come I had to fall in love with a non-Chinese man? Why another break-up?

"Now that you are staying with us, I will make sure that you eat and be happy. Don't worry too much about Yeng's health. Can't you see that she is fine now?" said my aunt.

My mother just gave my aunt a slight smile. Then, she was back to her world of oblivion again.

"Yeng, I think that your mother looks different this time than eight years ago," my uncle said to me the next day. "She seems to isolate herself. What is she like in Toronto?"

"Well, everyday, she would call me up. Afterwards, she would go to the corner of her street to buy her Chinese newspaper. Rain or shine, she would go. She never watches any television, except for the news. But lately, she told me that she is afraid of turning on the television because she fears that it might cause the apartment to catch fire. And she has stopped watching any television since then."

"Doesn't she have any friends?"

"Just a few from the church. But again, she would not call them up on her own. She tells me that she doesn't want to disturb them. But she would call me up at least six or seven times a day. If I don't call her up by ten in the evening, she would threaten me and tell me that she would lose sleep."

"I know that it's hard on you, Yeng. But try to be patient with her. Don't talk back to her. She is getting old now. She loves you very much," said my uncle.

"I know. That's why I just try my best to listen to her. I know she was extremely worried about me when I was sick in the hospital."

"Probably, if she had not moved to Toronto in the seventies, she would be a lot happier in Hong Kong," my aunt commented. "See, at least here, she knows Chinese and her way around. In Toronto, she doesn't. She has to rely on you. And with you sick in the hospital, it's tough for her."

"I know," I said. Yes, she might have been happier in Hong Kong, but me living in Toronto might have worried her too.

"That's why I would never immigrate to Canada at my age, as some of my friends do. Some of them moved to Canada because they were afraid of the takeover of Communist China. But now that Hong Kong is part of China, it is still so prosperous," said my uncle. "Hong Kong is so nice. Everything is within distance. The buses are frequent and there are mini-buses. Even taxis are easy to get. And I know the language and the people. There isn't any snow here either."

"That's right. Here in Hong Kong, I've lots of old friends whom I can have tea or play mahjong with," said my aunt. "Some of my friends want to go to Canada for its free medical care. But see, if I die, I die. It's all in God's plan."

We stayed at my uncle's apartment for about a month. Everyday, my uncle made chrysanthemum juice for me, bought milk for me, made dinner for us, and he even washed the dishes.

"Don't you do anything. You're on vacation. Wait until I go to Toronto, then, you will make dinner for me."

How ashamed I was! It should be the other way around because he is the senior of the family. I was really spoiled!

My aunt told me stories of my grandparents and my father, stories that I had never heard in the past. My mother sat there, listening intensely and joining in at times. My aunt told me that my grandparents were born in Taishan, a village in the Canton Province. Because of poverty, they moved to Hong Kong to improve their lot. When my father was sixteen years old, my grandfather died suddenly, leaving my grandmother, my two aunts, and my father. My father had to support them but, at the same time, had to study English and engineering on his own.

When he was about nineteen, he married the mother of my half sister. Then, he married my mother when he was about twenty-four.

Whenever my aunt talked about my father, my mother would smile with contentment. Did it mean that she still loved my father, though the marriage was not a very compatible and happy one? Or did it have to do with her traditional belief that a woman's fate, once married, was destined with her husband and his family? I was afraid to ask.

My uncle and my aunt took us to sweep the graves of my grandmother and my first mother. We took the mini-bus, then walked all the way to the cemetery. There I stood in front of their graves and bowed my head as a traditional way of showing respect. Yet I did not know my grandmother very well. She was about eighty-three when she moved in with us. I was in Grade Six then. She spoke only Taishanese, a Chinese dialect that I did not understand. Everyday, she would sit on the chair, counting her fingers, waiting to be fed by Amah Hing. Only now did I realize her loneliness, having to be surrounded by everyone in the household who could not understand her dialect. Though I never got to know my first mother who died of tuberculosis, my aunt told me that she was not happy, having had to marry to my father when she was eighteen out of an arranged marriage. Was her tuberculosis the result of her unhappiness, a somatic symptom for her depression? Perhaps. And perhaps, this was the plight of many Chinese women in her era, having to lead a life in social isolation, in emotional suppression, without the willpower or the ability to fight back against their fates.

My uncle and my aunt took us to the tourist areas of Hong Kong by the Mass Transit Railway. Modern and fast, this subway system had lots of trains running. We got off at the Tsim Sha Tsui Station on the Kowloon side. There were many boutiques, shops, and restaurants on the crowded Nathan Road. As we headed towards the Star Ferry Pier, the new Hong Kong Museum of Arts and the Art Centre, located just across from the famous Peninsula Hotel, were there. We took the Star Ferry across the Victoria Harbour to the Hong Kong Island. The Convention Centre protruded into the harbour. The National Flag of the Republic of China was hanging up high on the top of the Bank of China Tower. Other skyscrapers, the Central Plaza and the Hong Kong and Shanghai Bank, surrounded the tower in a distance. We then took the tram to the Victoria Peak, where we saw the breathtaking panoramic view of Hong Kong.

This was what I saw in the documentary when I was in the hospital. Now to see it in person was unbelievable. Yet somehow, I could not quite relate to this cosmopolitan city, this Pearl of the Orient, New York of the East, after living in Toronto for over twenty years. The pace of its lifestyle was too fast for me. The crowds appalled me. The jammed traffic scared me. Somehow, I lost the feeling of heritage with this city of my birth. I didn't feel much of a sense of belonging. Did it mean that I had changed? Perhaps. I could only see myself as an occasional visitor, trying to recapture my childhood.

It was Chinese New Year, the Year of the Tiger. My aunt's apartment was decorated with plum blossoms, happy wishes on red papers, a platter of oranges and tangerines, and a candy tray. On Chinese New Year's Eve, we had our dinner together with traditional Chinese New Year dishes—chicken, fish, bamboo shoots, Chinese mushrooms, and Chinese New Year cakes. It was the first time since my immigration to Canada in 1974 that I had my Chinese New Year dinner with my aunt and my uncle. It certainly brought back some of the happy memories of my childhood days. I was happier to spend Chinese New Year in Hong Kong than if I were in Toronto. In Toronto, the weather would be very cold with snow. And there would not be as much of a festive atmosphere as here.

After dinner, we went to the New Year's Fair down by Victoria Park, just about ten minutes by bus from their apartment. Tons of people, both young and old, were at the fair. Hawkers selling flowers of all kinds, toys, and candies were at their stalls, shouting loudly, trying to promote

Star Ferry in Hong Kong

their sales. There were palm readers and people writing poetic couplets with happy wishes on red papers. We bought some water lilies and narcissus.

Just as we were about to leave the park, there was the traditional Chinese New Year Dance—the colorful Dragon and Lion Dance with its rhythmic drumming and loud Chinese music. Suddenly, gorgeous fireworks of different shapes and colours burst into the sky, making the whole city become a magic land. The crowds, amazed by its surreal wonders, applauded and exclaimed in excitement.

New Year's Day came. My aunt prepared the traditional Chinese New Year dishes--sweet steamed glutinous rice pudding, a dish of vegetables, noodles, chicken, roasted pork, and rice. I ate them to my heart's delight. She then gave me the traditional lai-see, a red envelope with money that the elders give to the youngsters during the New Year.

"I hope that this New Year will bring you good health and happiness. Make sure that you listen to your mother and take your medications," she said.

I looked at her.

"I hope so too. I'll try."

My mother also gave me a lai-see. On the envelope, she wrote: "*My dear Yeng, good luck and good health. Your beloved Mom.*"

I was moved to tears. All at once, I could feel the love and the concern that my family had for me. They might not understand my illness and me very much. They might not be able to help me in the way that I had

wanted them to. And they might even think that my illness was a shame to the family. They were all human beings with their own limitations. Yet there they were, wishing me good luck and good health in their own way. This was what I called love. It was this recognition of love that had helped me to forge on and to combat my illness to the best of my ability.

Dear God, thank you
For the love of my mother,
My uncle, and my aunt.

From Victoria Peak - Hong Kong

Chapter twenty

YING WA GIRLS' REUNION

Besides my uncle and my aunt, the only other people whom I would like to see would be my good old girlfriends from my high school, Ying Wa Girls' School. I began to phone up my girlfriends.

"Is Chee Man there?"

"No, she's out," replied her Filipino maid.

"When will she be back?"

"In the afternoon, at around five or six."

"My name is Caroline Fei-Yeng. I've just come from Canada. Ask her to call me back at 2546-9873 once she gets home, OK?"

"Sure. I'll let her know."

I called another friend, King Cheung, who happened to be at home. She is a piano teacher.

"Hey, Fei-Yeng, are you in Hong Kong now?"

"Of course. I just arrived two days ago."

"Did you suffer from jet-lag?"

"No, I don't think so. I have been sleeping for at least eight hours for the past two nights. How's everybody?"

"They're fine. Suk Han now works as an educational psychologist again. Yuk-Chun works as the principal inspector with the Special Education Branch of the government. Wai Lim is a lecturer at the Hong Kong College of Technology and Management Association. Wai Ying works as a beauty consultant at a spa in a hotel. Wei Wong works at the Bank of America. Ka Lin is the manager of the Music Department of the government. You know Yuen Ting? She is a movie director. In fact, she has just directed a movie and we all went to her launch party. Chee Man flies between Hong Kong and England quite often to see her children. Mei Yee is back from Australia. And Ka Wah now lives in Hong Kong."

King Cheung was more excited than I on the phone. After all, we had known each other since we were in elementary school.

"How's your mother? Is she here with you? Remember how she cooked for us when I was in Toronto?"

Yes, I remembered the days when my mother used to cook for us on most weekends. That was about twenty years ago. King Cheung and her husband had since moved back to Hong Kong to live.

Just about when we finished the conversation, the telephone rang. It was Chee Man returning the call. Chee Man, a lawyer herself who is married and has two children, is one of my best friends to whom I had confided most of my secrets. When I was having my marital problems, she was the one who gave me emotional support and understanding. We had also done some traveling, visiting different countries in Europe on our own.

"Fei Yeng, this is Chee Man. My maid left a message in my voice mail. I'm calling you from the cell phone in my car. So, *you're* back in Hong Kong."

"Just wait, Chee Man. King Cheung is on the other line. I have to tell her to hang up first. Give me one second," I said. "Now, Chee Man, I can talk. How have you been? It's really exciting to hear your voice. When are we going to get together with the rest of the gang?"

"You've come at the right time. Our monthly get-together will be coming this Friday at a Chinese restaurant in Hong Kong Central. Make sure that you dress properly. I'll give you a ride, so you don't have to get a taxi."

The telephone rang again. This time, it was from Ka Lin. "Fei-Yeng, King Cheung just told me that you're in Hong Kong. Isn't it funny? Just this morning, I thought about you and now you're in Hong Kong."

"Well, maybe it's telepathy."

My uncle's apartment had suddenly become one of Bell Canada's offices and I had been transformed into the Chief Operator, handling all

the calls. Just like in my days in high school, I was a happy chatterbox once again.

These calls had brought back the real me, the lively and spontaneous me, that some doctors and colleagues did not understand. Perhaps, in their mind, Chinese women should sit still, be obedient, and never talk back. A submissive bunch, that is. At the same time, these phone calls reminded me of the pain that I went through at Mount Sinai Hospital in my previous admissions, where quarters were needed in order to make phone calls and, oftentimes, the nurses would interrupt my calls. No quarters, no calls. How inhuman! Patients, especially psychiatric patients, are most fragile. Why cannot they be given the right to call up their friends and relatives? Were the doctors afraid that their friends would be annoyed if the patients called them during office hours and disturbed their routine?

What are friends for anyway?

On Friday, I waited for Chee Man down by the entrance of my uncle's building. Out from the car came Chee Man in her beige suit with a matching woolen coat. We hadn't seen each other for about eight years. Except for her hair cut, she still looked the same to me.

"Hey, Fei Yeng, I'm so glad that you are visiting Hong Kong now. And you look great!!"

"Thanks. You too."

"Don't worry about your illness now. Just relax and have a good time with us in Hong Kong, OK? I will take you to the Marina Club to have a swim one day. We'll have a body message there."

The earnestness in her voice touched me.

At the restaurant, all of my girlfriends were there. They had already ordered some delicious dishes.

"Eat, Fei Yeng. You won't get such good food in Toronto." They kept giving me several servings.

At the end of the dinner, Wai Lim gave me a present.

"It is a present from all of us. We just want to let you know that though we're miles apart, we care about you very much."

I looked at her, wanting to say that I didn't deserve it.

"Open it, Fei Yeng."

I opened my present. It was a little glass baby grand piano. This display of sincerity was overwhelming to me. For a moment, I could not say a word.

"Thanks so much, everybody. Whenever I look at this piano, I will always think of you guys."

We talked about old times, childhood fun, and school gossip. Fond memories of time past. Sweet moments of innocence.

Chee Man took me to the Marina Club the next day. There I had a swim. Sitting by the poolside, Chee Man and I recalled when we entered the Hong Kong Music and Speech Festival and recited our poems. Slowly I recited my favorite lines in Wordsworth's poem, *Ode: Intimations of Immortality:*

> *"What though the radiance which was once so bright*
> *Be now forever taken from my sight,*
> *Though nothing can bring back the hour*
> *Of splendor in the grass, of glory in the flower;*
> *We will grieve not, rather find*
> *Strength in what remains behind."*

Chee Man was amazed that I could remember them all. Yet she did not know that it was these lines that had kept me going when I was in the hospital.

Yuen Ting also took me to the Repulse Bay Hotel to have an afternoon tea. Sitting on the porch of the hotel and looking at the gorgeous

Repulse Bay brought back many long-lost childhood memories.

"Remember how we wrote our movie plots every day during lunch hours on the blackboard?" said Yuen Ting.

"Sure, I do. Maybe that's what made you become a movie director now."

The Repulse Bay had changed from years ago. There on the beach were the two new Chinese goddess sculptures—Kwun Yum and Tin Hau. The beach itself had become more and more polluted with litter all around. Then we drove to the Stanley Market at nearby Stanley Beach. It was in this market where Chinese paintings and souvenirs for tourists were sold.

Yuen Ting, Chee Man, and I also spent a day visiting my Amah Hing. Amah Hing had moved to live with her daughter, son-in-law, and two grandsons after my parents had immigrated to Canada. She had been my amah since I was twenty days old. When I was little, she took me to school everyday, holding my hand. She made all the dresses for me. With my mother working in my father's firm all day, I was close to my Amah Hing in many ways. I especially liked her smiles and her gentle voice. We listened to the radio shows and saw Chinese movies together. And I confided in her some of my secrets at school. She knew all my girlfriends from my school. She was, indeed, like a second mother to me and I was like a daughter to her. She buried herself and cried for days when I went to study in the States.

She lives in the Wong Tai Sin area. Children were playing in the area while some seniors were sitting on the bench outside. We climbed up to the seventh floor and knocked at the door. Amah Hing opened the iron barred door. In we went to the apartment. It was an extremely small apartment of about two hundred square feet with two double bunk beds and lots of bags and luggage hanging around. There was a wooden bench across the room.

"Come on in, Yeng, Chee Man, and Yuen Ting. It's small, but five of us live here," she said, embarrassed. "So how have you been, Yeng? You seem to have gained some weight. See, my legs. I can't walk well these days."

She wanted to pour us some tea, but as she walked, she wobbled.

"Did you see a doctor? What did the doctor say?" I asked.

"The doctor says that I'm fine. Just old age. Take some vitamins and I'm fine."

"How can you climb these stairs?"

"I stay home," she said. "Come, Yeng, I've knitted a blanket for you to take back to Canada. The weather there is cold. I know. Remember in December 1981, your father took me to visit you in Toronto?"

Me, Yuen Ting and Chee Man

She smiled.

"Yes, I sure do. We went to Niagara Falls, CN Tower, the Eaton Centre, and restaurants in Chinatown, remember?"

"Yes. Those were the days. I still have the pictures," she said as she got the picture that I took with her in Niagara Falls from her wallet. "You and I really looked great, don't you think?"

She looked at the picture in nostalgia and with great delight.

"We did," said I. Yes, the picture was taken about seventeen years ago. I had been divorced and my father had died since then. Looking at Amah Hing now, she had also aged with white hair and wrinkles. Perhaps I had aged too.

"Amah Hing, you should take good care of yourself too. Here is my gift to you for the New Year." I gave her $500 wrapped in a Chinese New

Year red envelope.

Amah Hing

"You shouldn't. I've enough money to survive."

She didn't want to take it.

"Take it. It's good luck. I probably won't be back for a long time."

At that moment, I had to rush out of her apartment. I could not hold back my tears seeing my beloved Amah Hing having to live in such conditions. Just like my mother, I did not want her and my friends to see my emotions displayed.

This was my last time seeing Amah Hing. She died in 2000 of Alzheimer's Disease in a nursing home in Hong Kong. But her hand-knitted blanket would forever stay with me.

One afternoon, Yuk Chun drove me to the New Territories after having breakfast at the Hong Kong Jockey Club. We stopped by at a place where there was a make-a-wish tree. I wrote my secret wish on a piece of red paper, wrapped it with an orange and then threw it high into a tree. We also visited the Castle Peak Psychiatric Hospital. The buildings of the hospital were extremely modern. There, the tour leader showed us some of their facilities: the computer room, the art room, the factory room, and the tuck shop operated by the patients themselves. We also visited one of the patients' rooms. The room itself was nicely decorated and there were ten beds, each with an end table, in the room. The patients were, on the whole, friendly and quite articulate.

As we had our hospital visit, I asked Yuk Chun, who worked with the mental health field in Hong Kong, a question that I found puzzling.

"Yuk Chun, now that I've been in Hong Kong for about three weeks, there has been at least three to four cases of people committing suicides. Seems like that there are more cases in Hong Kong than in Toronto. Why?"

"Probably because of the economic pressure. See, in 1997, there was a sudden decline in real estate here. Maybe other reasons too. Marital break-ups, unemployment, and undetected mental illnesses. You know something? Many people are ignorant and ashamed of being diagnosed as mentally ill. So they don't seek help until it becomes too late. Besides, there is a lack of social support and understanding for the mentally ill too."

I became silent. I was lucky then. Had my principal not told me to seek help and assured me of my financial stability with the school board, I might not have sought help and became seriously sick.

On another day, Chee Man, Yuen Ting, Wai Ying, and I went to Macau together. Macau is an island, a Portuguese colony until 1999, which takes about an hour by hydrofoil from Hong Kong. The narrow streets in Macau, with its old, three story buildings and non-air-conditioned buses, reminded me of Hong Kong in the fifties. Had I gone back to the days when I was growing up in Hong Kong? There we went to its famous Casinos, visited the Cathedral, Dr. Sun Yat-Sen Memorial Museum, and had its famous Portuguese chicken in Taipa Island. We also had our coffee in the modern Starbuck Coffee Shop.

Ka Wah, Wei Wong, Suk Han, Ka Lin, and Mei Yee also took me to shop at Times Square in Causeway Bay. It was a huge plaza with restaurants, boutiques, music stores, sportswear shops, and a a supermarket on several floors. I was particularly interested in the supermarket, where they have foods from different countries of the world. Hong Kong is, indeed, a cosmopolitan city with many facets of activities and lifestyles.

The most memorable night was the evening when we all went to Club Fifties in Lan Kwai Fong in Hong Kong Central, just a few nights before I left. Lan Kwai Fong is a trendy nightlife haunt in Central Hong Kong Island with more than fifty restaurants and clubs.

me, Yuen Ting, Wai Ying, Chee Man in Macau

For the first time, I sang Karaoke in a club! We sang songs that we used to sing in our folk song group when we were in high school—*Yellow Bird*, *Jamaica Farewell*, *The Cruel War*, *Puff the Magic Dragon*, and *Lemon Tree*. Suddenly, I became young again. I became a high school student, dressed in my blue school uniform, performing on the stage in front of my fellow mates. All the glorious days came back to me—the weekly rehearsals, the anxiety of stage fright, and the eventual applause from the audience.

We ended up the night by holding hand and singing the song, *The Light of Friendship*, in Chinese:

> *"In our lives in this world,*
> *How many are true and caring friends?*
> *How many friendships are long-lasting?*
> *When we were separated*
> *from each other yesterday,*
> *We were holding each other's hands,*
> *Our friendship is long-lasting in our hearts.*
> *Today, we may have to be separated*
> *for a short while,*

We will be together some day.
Even though we can't see each other,
We are still friends forever.
Let's say there are lots of mountains,
And lots of lands that separate us,
We don't have to see each other,
We know from our hearts,
That our true friendship will never change."

Each of my girlfriends leads a different life-style: some single, some married, and some divorced. Some are housewives and some are professionals. Yet every month all through these years, they gather together at different restaurants, chitchatting about old times, exchanging greetings, and supporting one another. Isn't this what long lasting friendship is all about?

Abraham Lincoln emancipated the slaves. My Ying Wa girlfriends emancipated me, the depressed me who, for years, had to suppress my feelings and emotions under the name of manic-depression. Their warmth did more than any medications to help heal my illness. For years, I did not have any friends whom I could relate to

Friends in Hong Kong

so well and to share my feelings with. With them, no more tears. No more sorrows. Only laughter, jokes, and stories. With them, I could be free to recite my poems and to sing the songs. All of a sudden, I felt that I was not an ugly duckling anymore, but a beautiful swan, gliding along the pond on Centre Island in Lake Ontario.

They all knew about my illness and my family situation. Yet did they call me Ms. Crazy or the Retard? No. Instead, through their sincerity and positive beliefs in me, they gave me the courage and the support to fight against manic-depression.

Dear God, thank you
For giving me such
Good and caring friends.

my friends in Hong Kong

Chapter twenty-one

GOOD MORNING, BEIJING

The flight attendant of China Airlines announced in Mandarin: "Good morning, ladies and gentlemen, we are about to land at Beijing's International Airport in five minutes. Please fasten your seatbelts until the signal is turned off. Thank you for your cooperation."

the Great Wall

Both my mother and I peeped through the window. Skyscrapers among rice paddies and country roads. Is this Beijing, the Capital of the People's Republic of China? It was my first time to ever set foot on this motherland of mine. My mother started to hum her favorite song, the National Anthem of China:

> *"Arise, ye who refused to be slaves,*
> *with our flesh and blood,*
> *let us build our new Great Wall..."*

Suddenly, it reminded me of my own display of my patriotism when I was singing the same anthem in the hospital—a behavior that, according to Nurse Cheryl and Dr. Yiu, was inappropriate.

The roads from the airport to the hotel were literally filled with bicycles, cars, and taxis. Bicycles and tricycles squeezed in every corner. Cars and taxis honked at one another. And people! Throngs strolled along the roads; buses were jammed. And there were hardly any traffic lights!

The tour bus dropped us off at the Crown Plaza Hotel, located in a tourist area on Wangfungjing Avenue. A five-star hotel, the guide told us. It was very luxurious with a chandelier, carpets, a swimming pool, bars, restaurants, sauna, and steam bath rooms. Very modernized telephones, too. It looked as if I were in an expensive hotel in Paris' Champs Elyseese, rather than in a hotel in Communist China.

The tour group consisted of about thirty people. All were Chinese from different parts of the world—Hong Kong, Holland, Canada, the United States, and the United Kingdom. A true global village.

We visited many historical sites. Standing outside of the Great Wall National Theatre at the Great Wall in Badaling, I saw the majestic view of the Great Wall. I was equally impressed by the Forbidden City; the roofs were built in yellow glazed tiles while the inside of the palace was painted in yellow with grand decorations and paintings along its deluxe halls. In the Summer Palace are Kunming Lake, Back Lake, and West Lake, which are connected with bridges. It has many imperial gardens, one of which is The Garden of Harmonious Interests, which has a long corridor of exquisite color paintings linked with the buildings and the garden. We also visited the Tiananmen Square. At the centre of the Square is the Monument to the People's Heroes; north is the Tiananmen Tower; west is the Great Hall of the People; and south is the Mao ZeDong Memorial Hall. In the Memorial Hall is Mao ZeDong in a crystal coffin surrounded by fresh bouquets of various famous flowers and grasses.

the Summer Palace - Beijing

Having been raised in the Colonial days of Hong Kong, I did not

study or know much about China or its history. In our history syllabus, we had to study the history of England. As for Chinese history, there was little mention of the many developments in China. I was confused with the different dynasties, and did not know much about the Cultural Revolution. When I was in front of these great architectural sites, I was at a loss. How ashamed I was that I knew so little of China, my motherland.

The only significant event that I could relate to was the Chinese Democratic Movement on June 4, 1989 in the Tiananmen Square, which ended in bloodshed when the People's Liberation Army killed at least 2600 students and wounded thousands. As I was standing at the Square, I could visualize the torments that these young, rebellious souls had gone through. Just like psychiatric patients, their voices were suppressed in their fight for their rights.

Yes, the June 4 Movement in 1989. For the first time, I participated in a candlelight vigil at the Nathan Phillip Square in downtown Toronto. For the first time, I sensed the unity of overseas Chinese in their cries for justice. And for the first time, I realized the patriotism of my mother when she bowed to the dead with a carnation in front of the Chinese Consulate on St. George Street.

My mother, on the contrary, was very excited about these historical sites. During the tours, she listened attentively to the tour guide's explanations. And in spite of the crowds and her age, she managed to walk much faster than me. She told me stories of her past that I had never heard before, of how she used to be in the Chinese medical team, helping the wounded, when Japan invaded China. Her eyes beamed with pride as she recounted these stories in nostalgia. All of a sudden, her youthful and energetic self seemed to have replaced her apathetic self. Perhaps this tour had liberated her mind from her worries about my illness, and instead had brought back her old and fond memories of her younger days.

We had our meals in different restaurants. Peking duck with dumplings, deep-fried Shanghai noodles and soybean soup were all very

delicious. Unlike her isolated self in Toronto, my mother initiated conversations with the tour members. She talked about practically everything—from weather, to Canada, to her grandchildren. I was surprised. For once, she was happy. And for once, she had an audience. Had I neglected her needs in Toronto? Or had she not adjusted to the living style in Toronto, of having to be surrounded by people who do not share and understand her culture and language? Or had seeing me suffer in the hospital made her feel guilty about herself?

Before we left Beijing, I called up the mother of my former piano teacher. In my broken Mandarin, I told her that her daughter, Shao Han, was my piano teacher. She was delighted and excited. "Where is your hotel? I'm going to get a taxi cab to come to your hotel and meet you."

About an hour later, she was already at our hotel. There, she, my mother, and I had tea in the café. Like my mother, she was a skinny lady with white hair. She was seven-eight years old, she told us. Dressed in a traditional navy suit, she looked older than her age.

"I look old, I know. But see, I am not as lucky as you. I had to go through the Cultural Revolution in the late sixties and had to bring up Shao Han by myself."

"Why?" I asked.

"Because my husband was killed in the Revolution," she said and then paused. She changed the tone of her voice. "Well, it's all over now. The hard times are gone. These days, I am happy that I have a one-bedroom government apartment. At least, these days, I have food to eat. And Shao Han sends me money every month."

She smiled when she talked about Shao Han.

"How is she doing in Toronto anyway? Is she happy? Does she have a lot of students? And many friends?"

"She is doing fine. She has at least twenty students every week. And she is also busy with lots of other cultural activities. She just gave a recital at the University of Toronto in March last year. I was there. She played Tchaikovsky, Beethoven, and Bach. And there was a standing ovation at the end. Don't worry, Mrs. Han."

"That's good. I pray to Buddha every day for her. I haven't seen her for over five years now. She only calls once a month. You're lucky, Mrs. Kwok, that your daughter is with you."

"Maybe, Mrs. Han," said my mother. "I pray to God for my daughter, too."

They looked at each other and exchanged a smile, a smile of consolation.

"When you get back to Toronto, tell Shao Han to take good care of herself. Ask her to call me twice a month. I will pay for the phone bill. And ask her to put on a sweater. The weather in Toronto must be very chilly now."

"I will, Mrs. Han."

"Here is a little something for you. Take it."

"You don't have to, Mrs. Han."

"Open it. I got it for you." I opened it. It was a little wooden Buddha pendant. I was thrilled by her friendly gesture. Immediately, I put it around my neck. As we were about to say good-bye, she asked me once again to tell Shao Han to dress warm.

Her concerns for her daughter reminded me so much of my mother. Nagging. Yet on second thought, it is motherly love. In spite of my occasional outbursts to my mother and her lack of understanding of my illness, she still loves me, just like Mary loves Jesus. Mary held Jesus on her lap after He was taken down from the Cross. So is my mother holding me in her own way each and every day, helping me to recover from my illness to the best of her ability. Perhaps I had misinterpreted her concern as nagging. Or is her love for me too intense and so strong that it has become a psychological burden to me? Whatever it is, I now realize that the strong bond between mothers and their children is beyond boundaries. It is a natural blessing from God.

After I took a shower that night, I lay on my bed. My mother did not know that I was still awake. She came to my bed, put a blanket over me,

and then walked back to her bed.

After a while, she was asleep. I looked at my mother's tiny body and aging face once again. Good night, mother, my Sleeping Beauty.

Dear God,
Thank you for
My trip to my motherland.

Chapter twenty-two

FAREWELL, HONG KONG

It was my last night in Hong Kong. I took the Star Ferry that runs across Fragrant Harbour from the Kowloon side to Hong Kong Island. There were many boats and tankers at the harbour and the water was turbulent with splashing waves. It reminded me of a piano piece that I played, *The Waves of the Ocean.* When would I see this harbour again? And the neon lights of the skyscrapers? I remembered one of my favorite poems, *Sea Fever,* by John Masefield:

> *"I must go down to the seas again,*
> *to the lonely sea and the sky,*
> *and all I ask is a tall ship,*
> *and a star to steer her by…"*

In Toronto, there are only lakes and rivers. Oh, South China Sea, after tonight, I can only dream about you from a distance. Look at the dark sky! And the full moon and the stars! They were all good signs. Will fortune and happiness be waiting for me in Toronto? Who knows? Yet this golden moment of joy will forever be a reminder of my days in this birthplace of mine. Yes, Hong Kong, my beloved Hong Kong.

But somehow, I also felt that I no longer belonged to Hong Kong. I could not recognize most of the streets and the buildings. I was like a lone traveler who had lost her direction in her journey. The negative experience of my hospitalization in Hong Kong years ago still haunted me.

A visitor I had become. I looked at this Pearl of the Orient with fond memories of my younger days, days when I was healthy and happy. Yes, I remembered my high school, located right at mid-level, overlooking the harbour. Every morning, I went down to Silcock's Hall with my class-

mates in my navy blue Cheung Sam uniform for our morning assembly. There, we sang hymns and listened to talks by our teachers.

In my class of about thirty students, I studied subjects ranging from the Bible, to English, to Chinese Literature. I joined in activities after school–Drama Club, Exploration Club and the Literary and Debating Club. Every Saturday after school, I would go to the British Council Library down by Hong Kong Downtown Central to read magazines and newspapers with my classmates.

Those were the days. And in those days, there were not a lot of sky-scrapers like there are now. The air was not so polluted and the water in the harbour was cleaner.

As the Star Ferry was approaching the Hong Kong Island Pier, I looked back at the Kowloon Pier. The big red clock was still standing stoically. The Ocean Terminal was there. The Hong Kong Art Centre and the Hong Kong Museum of Arts were there. At one of the docks was a big cruise ship. All of a sudden, I thought of Ophelia in Shakespeare's *Hamlet* saying:

"Good night, ladies, good night,
Sweet ladies, good night, good night."

People rushed out of the ferry, as if they were refugees in a war zone. I was the last to leave the ferry. In my heart, I quietly said, "Good night, Hong Kong. Good night. God bless my homeland."

I took a taxi back to my uncle's apartment through the jammed Hen-nessy Road in the Causeway Bay area. Sogo, the big department store, was filled with shoppers. The trams and the colorful double-decker buses crowded the road. Neon lights of the restaurants and shops lit up the streets. This excitement on the streets certainly added to the bustling and dynamic flavour of this cosmopolitan city.

When I reached my uncle's apartment, to my surprise, my aunt had already prepared three Taishanese dishes for my mother and me. A farewell dinner, of course. Immediately, I got my camera out and took a shot of the three dishes. All of them--fried shrimps, stir-fry vegetables, and fish—are my favorites. Would this be the Last Supper? Who knows? The next day, my mother and I would be on the plane. Would I be able to see these old folks again? My aunt seemed to understand my mood very well. She looked at me and assured me, "Don't worry, Yeng. We *will* see each other again. I'm healthy and strong. Just take good care of yourself, and listen to your doctors. Take good care of your mother and remember, don't talk back to her."

Jammed traffic in Hong Kong

At dinner, my aunt started to tell me the old folk tales of the Taishan Village where my ancestors lived, that the village was very poor, that many people did not have much education. Just like when I was in Beijing, I felt ashamed again. I did not even know how to speak the Taishanese dialect. But at the same time, I felt that I was lucky that my grandparents fled to Hong Kong and that I could have a good education.

After dinner, my uncle went to his room and gave me a gold pen engraved with the words "*courage and determination*" in Chinese.

"Take this pen. It's my gift to you. Use it to write good stories so that you will be recognized as a top writer one of these days. Don't ever give up this dream of yours. I know that you can do it. But remember always that your ancestors are from China and you are Chinese. Try to be nice to your mother, though I know it's hard at times. But she loves you more than anyone else in this world. And make sure that you take the medications, then, you'll be alright."

I was overwhelmed with emotion. I looked at him, then the pen, and said thank you with a lump in my throat. Just then, the telephone rang. It was Chee Man.

"Hey, Fei Yeng, I just want to say good-bye. Don't worry about your job. When your health is fine, I'm sure that the school board will let you go back to work again. Even if they don't let you go back, that's not the end of the world. There will probably be some better opportunities waiting for you elsewhere. Maybe you will end up as an actress! Remember you got the Garrison Trophy as Prospero in *The Tempest* at the Hong Kong Music and Speech Festival years ago? Many actresses are manic-depressives, you know."

"Who are they?"

"Marilyn Monroe, for sure, and Vivien Leigh, too."

"But I will never be like them, to commit suicide."

"I know you wouldn't. I've known you for so many years. I know that you're too chicken to kill yourself," Chee Man teased me.

She was right. I am always afraid of death. Even in the moments of my utmost despair, the thought of committing suicide never occurred to me. Life is so interesting. Why waste it?

"You know what your problem is, Fei Yeng? You're too panicky at times when you face your emotional problems with men. You don't know how to cope with those situations. Perhaps your emotional quotient is a bit below average," she laughed.

"It's true, Chee Man."

"Change your philosophy. Be more realistic in your expectations with men. Then, you won't be disappointed."

"Then, I must have to learn those tricks from you, eh?" I teased her right back.

"Is that right? Well, don't think of Phillip all that much. Past is past. Concentrate on the present. You've to take good care of yourself. You're still young and attractive. Maybe you'll find a better man in the future."

"I know, but I still think of Phillip quite a bit. I have to learn to let go. It's hard work. Probably it takes time. Whenever I am in the psychiatrist's office, I become frozen. Oftentimes, I can't find the right word to describe my feelings about Phillip. What I do need are some understanding friends whom I can talk to about my relationship with him. I'll write to you when I get back. I've to go and pack now."

"You know something, Fei Yeng? If the school board is still sticky, come back to Hong Kong. There are lots of opportunities here. Besides, you've got a lot of good friends who grew up with you and truly care for you."

"I know, Chee Man. Thanks for your concern. But I don't think I can adjust back to Hong Kong again. The pace of life in Hong Kong is too fast for me. I am a manic-depressive. I still think that there is quite a lot of social stigma towards mental illness in Hong Kong. And you know what many Chinese are like? They think that mental illness is a shame, that it is a loss of face to the family. So there is a strong taboo against it. In Canada, social stigma exists, but it's not that great in comparison. There are more support groups in Canada. Besides, I get financial protection from my school board. Were I to become sick in Hong Kong, I could not afford to see doctors. Don't forget that I also have a thyroid problem and I'm a diabetic. I also find that the cost of living in Hong Kong is much higher than Toronto."

"Well, just be calm. Anyway, be nice to your mother. This time when I saw her, she has really aged. See, she is getting old with her own problems too. And she cannot speak English. If you can't handle her, seek help from Dr. Wong. He is Chinese from

Free to Fly in Hong Kong

Hong Kong and has been your family physician for years. I heard that he is sympathetic to the Chinese seniors, isn't he?"

"Yes. He is a caring doctor."

"So both you and your mother are in good hands. By the way, don't trust all the psychiatrists. Some are real fruitcakes. I was reading in the newspaper the other day that psychiatrists have the highest divorce and suicide rates. Besides, I don't think that any of your psychiatrists have ever been to Hong Kong and know the way we were brought up?

"Is that right? Well, don't think of Phillip all that much. Past is past. Concentrate on the present. You've to take good care of yourself. You're still young and attractive. Maybe you'll find a better man in the future."

"Just call me or King Cheung or Yuen Ting, or Suk Han up, if you feel like talking about Phillip, or if you feel lonely at times. If you don't have enough money, just call collect. I promise I will accept the call. Don't worry, OK? Say hello to your mother for me."

"I will. Thanks, Chee Man. Remember, I have always been a fighter, even in my high school days. Don't worry about my job situation. I trust my principal, Mr. Dick, and the teachers' union too. All I have to do is to learn to be more emotionally detached, develop my coping skills when faced with adversities, and have more interests and hobbies besides teaching. To improve my emotional quotient, that is."

"That's an excellent idea. I'm sure you'll be able to do that. You're a woman of guts."

"OK. Good-bye. I really have to pack now. Send my regards to your husband and children. And your in-laws too."

By the time I got off the phone, it was already midnight. Everyone was asleep. There was a full moon in the sky. And the stars too. A light of hope for my future? Good night, my friends. And farewell, Hong Kong.

Dear God,
Bless my Hong Kong,
My aunt, my uncle,
And my friends.
Thank you.

Chapter twenty-three

REFLECTIONS

The flight to Toronto was a long one. My mother was fast asleep, but I could not sleep. There was a tumultuous commotion on the plane.

My mind went back to the summer of 1980 when I flew long distance from Hong Kong to Toronto alone. I could not sleep then. More so, I was agitated and distressed. I had not had any sleep for several nights. Why? Because Wilbert and I had a terrible fight over the phone.

I had gone back to Hong Kong that summer with my parents. Wilbert had agreed to it. We had also planned to go on a cruise to Alaska afterwards. My reasons for going back to Hong Kong had partly to do with my two month long vacation from teaching, but mainly because I wanted to have some time off by myself to think about my relationship with Wilbert. My relationship with him had deteriorated since 1978.

When I first came to Toronto in 1974, I had to take a Bachelor of Education degree to retrain myself for my "Canadian experience." I was placed teaching Business Education in a vocational school with the Toronto District School Board. I did not like the subject at all and could not imagine myself teaching it for the rest of my life. I then had an evening job, two evenings a week, with the school board, coordinating and teaching English as a Second Language in the then-pilot bilingual (Chinese and English) program. On top of that, I also enrolled myself part time in a graduate program at the Ontario Institute for Studies in Education of the University of Toronto, majoring in Second Language Teaching and Minority Education.

Wilbert also had to retrain himself to get his Canadian experience after he lost his job as a marketing representative with one of the oil companies in Toronto. He then had to work a full-time job and take three accounting courses in the evening.

On top of the fact that we did not share a lot of common interets to begin with, this situation left little time for us to enrich ourselves as a couple. We did not have many friends either, being new to Toronto. In 1977, my parents came to Canada and came to live with us. My relationship with Willburt became worse, and of course, there were conflicts and fights. By 1978, after Willburt got his accounting degree, he wanted to move out.

The Alaskan cruise never came to a reality. Instead, knowing that I could not handle the emotional stress of our relationship, I signed myself in at the North York General Hospital right after I landed in Toronto, hoping to get professional help for my relationship with Wilbert and myself. Having been exhausted by my long distance travel, I was crying in distress and rambling in my accented English in a very quick manner. It was there that the psychiatrist formally diagnosed me as a manic-depressive.

According to the medical record, the psychiatrist gave me lithium, methotrimeprazine, sodium amytol, haloperidol, and chlorpromazaine. Yet he wrote that my behaviour remained very active, uncooperative, and demanding, that I had a good relationship with my parents, and that Wilbert appeared to be extremely tolerant and supportive. In my three months of hospitalization there, the psychiatrist did not notice that I was unhappy in my marriage. He was also surprised that in spite of my phone calls to the school board, I could still have my teaching job.

I eventually divorced Wilbert in 1982.

"Miss, do you want some juice?" The flight attendant disturbed my train of thought.

"Yes, please."

After I sipped my juice, I was in nostalgia again.

This time, it was in July of 1992. My relationship with a colleague ended abruptly shortly before the end of the school term. I had planned my trip to London, England for a few weeks. Not understanding the extent of the emotional trauma, I went to London alone. I tried to reach

some of my friends in England, but could not. The Holiday Inn sent me to the psychiatric ward of the Whittington General Hospital on Highgate Hill in the inner city of London.

Unlike the emergency departments in Toronto's hospitals, the emergency department there was not spacious and only had some old furniture and a dying plant. I was in a panic with tears dripping over my face. A nurse kindly gave me a tissue.

"Can I call Toronto?" I asked.

"No, you can't until you've been admitted," said the nurse with a comforting voice. "Don't worry. You'll be alright."

Two nurses and a doctor walked with me from the emergency department through an open space to the ward. On our way, I requested that I be allowed to sing a song in order to relax myself. We all joined our hands and started singing the hymn, *"Stand up, stand up for Jesus."*

The next day, at the doctor's office, I called Dr. Wong up in Toronto. He had only been my family physician for about a year then. He was shocked.

"What happened?"

"I was emotionally distressed because of this sudden split up with my friend. I was at the Holiday Inn, crying alone. I also ran out of money."

"Did you spend a lot of money?"

"No, not really. It's just that I did not know that I have exceeded the limit of my credit card."

"Did you pay the Holiday Inn for your stay?"

"I did. Just managed."

"Have you ever thought of committing suicide?"

"Of course not," I answered positively. "Can you contact my mother to send me some money? I need it."

"Sure, I'll do that. Don't worry. Everything will be fine. Why don't you let me speak to your doctors there?"

Unlike the wards in Toronto, the psychiatric ward there was very old with several floors to it. The doctor's office on my floor was tiny with lots of files lying around. The patients' rooms were very small too. A bathroom with a big bath and a shower were shared among the patients. There was a dining area down on the first floor where all the patients would assemble for every meal served. The food there was delicious: sometimes waffles for breakfast; spaghetti for lunch; and meat pies with peas for dinner. And every afternoon, high tea was served. Barbecues were held in the small courtyard outside the kitchen area. There was also a tuck shop where candies and other accessories were sold. Outside the psychiatric wing were a tennis court and a library where books could be borrowed.

One of the inmates was an American lady who had been in the hospital for forty years. The other one was a Chinese woman from Hong Kong who told me in Cantonese that she was deserted by her husband and had been in the hospital for over five years. She felt that her chance of getting out was very slim. Another inmate was an elderly, blind man. Maria was another young inmate who gave me a comb when she was released.

I was scared that I might have to be locked up for the rest of my life. I asked my primary nurse, David.

"No, you won't. Don't worry. Each of the patients here is different. I can assure you that you will be out very soon."

Did I have the courage to express my doubt? If I did, he might think that I was paranoid. That would have added another symptom to my illness. Of course, I just hid my feelings.

The nurses there were warm and friendly. One male nurse, George, taught me how to dance after dinner. Another nurse, Amanda from Ireland, played the National Anthem of Ireland with me on the broken piano down in the basement, singing our hearts out. The music therapist, Michael, encouraged me to beat the drums as loudly as I could. The social worker, David, was always there whenever I needed some help in the carpentry program or when I needed some mental health information. He encouraged me to write a book about mental illness one day.

Just like most of the psychiatrists in Toronto, the psychiatrists there remained distant and detached.

I had my daily pass to go out of the hospital within a few days. There was a Chinese restaurant down by Highgate Hill called Lai Yuen Restaurant. I went there for lunch and chatted with the owner, Wai Leung Lai, and his friend, Wah. They were very sympathetic to me and offered to give me free meals every day. We shared a lot of jokes and laughs there, talking about China and Hong Kong. I found out that Wah was from China and Wai Leung Lai was from the New Territories in Hong Kong. Wah would cook for me delicious fried rice and noodles. They even called my mother up and paid for the calls.

I was lucky to have run into them who, though being strangers, had become my friends at the moment when I needed friendship most. Their sincerity and generosity really made me feel accepted in spite of my illness. I was also lucky that they made me feel at home as if I were in Toronto with my friends.

My two girlfriends, Chee Man and Wai Lim, who were in England then, visited me one afternoon. I had not seen Chee Man for three years and Wai Lim since we had left high school. They were appalled when they saw me in such bad shape. They tried to cheer me up by telling me stories of our high school days.

"Come on, Fei Yeng, cheer up. Think of our good old days in Ying Wa," said Wai Lim. "Remember how we changed our classroom for Ms. Pilkington's class on April Fool's Day? And how the whole class boycotted this Chinese Literature teacher by refusing to eat his treats?"

Laughter.

Indeed, we really were a naughty bunch. In all my years of teaching in Hong Kong and in Toronto, never had I encountered students such as us.

"Fei Yeng. Just think of our good old days. And don't think of this colleague of yours too much. He has hurt you, so why do you still have to think of him, right?" said Chee Man. "Be strong. Take control of your life and your emotions. Take my advice. Sometimes, one can enjoy oneself much better with girlfriends than with men. Don't you agree, Wai Lim?"

"I certainly do."

Their visit had certainly brightened up my life in a hospital miles away from home. It was, indeed, a consolation to know the concern and the warmth of my long-time friends.

The money from my mother arrived. To my surprise, only two checks of sixty Canadian dollars each came. The weather in England was getting cooler. I did not even have enough money to buy any winter clothes.

I contacted the Canadian Embassy without letting the hospital staff know. On one rainy day, when I had my pass, I went to the Embassy and arranged to have a meeting with one of the officers. I was soaking wet from top to bottom.

"I am a Canadian Citizen and I am a teacher with the Toronto District School Board. I am also a manic-depressive who has become ill while on holiday here. My plane ticket to Toronto has already expired. I want to go home…" I said, distraught. Tears rolled down my cheek.

"Don't worry. I'll arrange for you to go home once I have contacted the hospital staff. When they say that it is fine for you to travel, then, you will be able to go home," consoled the officer. "How did you get to our office?"

"By subway. I looked at the map and asked around."

She looked at me with amazement.

A few days later, I had an interview with the psychiatrist who gave me an OK to go back to Toronto. The hospital had to find an "escort" with a Canadian passport to take me back.

There I was on my way to Canada. When I arrived at the airport, my brother Bill was there, waiting to pick me up.

"Ladies and gentlemen, we will land at Toronto Pearson International Airport in about half an hour. Please fasten your seat belts and no smok-

ing is allowed," announced the captain.

Outside, the sky was dark. My mother was awakened by the announcement. My thought was interrupted too.

"Where are we?" She asked.

"We're in Toronto now. We're going to be home very soon."

She looked at me and held my hands in silence. I looked back at her. We exchanged a glance and we both smiled. Yes, safe and sound, to Toronto, my adopted city, once again.

Dear God, thank you,
For my memories.

Chapter twenty-four

HOME SWEET HOME

The plane finally touched down at the airport at around eight-thirty in the evening. After baggage claim, my mother and I went to the exit door. The airport was not as crowded as the airport in Hong Kong. Immediately, I saw Catherine and her husband, Donald, waving at us.

"Welcome home, Caroline. Come this way. Our car is over there," said Catherine.

"Thanks for picking us up. How's the weather?"

"We had a heavy snowstorm just about two days ago. You're so lucky to have missed it. It's still a bit slushy out. Donald, take the luggage to the car. We'll be there in a minute," said Catherine. "So tell me, how's Hong Kong?"

"It's as crowded as always. Lots of new buildings and luxurious hotels. Doesn't look like the Hong Kong I used to know. Many shops with expensive clothes. Lots of excitement in the city of course. Same as in the colonial days, at least on the surface. It doesn't seem like a city in a communist country at all. "

"That's what many people told me. They also said that a lot of the young ones from Canada go back to Hong Kong and China to work because they can't find any jobs here. It's a pity that Canada is having its brain drain, not only to the States, but to Asia too," said Catherine. "Do you like Beijing?"

"Yes and no. See, I don't understand much about Chinese history. But I found the city very interesting and the historical sites were impressive."

"Oh, Donald's car is here. Come, Auntie. Let's get into the car."

As we were on our way to my house, we passed by the Queen Elizabeth Way. We hit the Lakeshore Boulevard where, to the right, was Lake Ontario. In a distance was the CN Tower standing stoically with the

Skydome next to it. There was hardly a soul on the streets. I thought of the crowded Victoria Harbour and the Star Ferry Pier in Hong Kong. Yes, here I was back to the quiet Toronto once again.

Our car then turned to Spadina Avenue and came to Dundas Street where Chinatown is. Neon lights with big Chinese characters brightened the dull streets in this winter night. Some of the restaurants were still open, but, unlike the restaurants in Hong Kong, they did not have many customers. This Chinatown is only a miniature of Hong Kong.

The car was warm with the heat on. But more so, the car was warm with friendship and concern. How many friends would give me a ride home late at night? And in this wintry weather? When I was sick in the hospital, Catherine visited me right after her return from attending her mother's funeral in China. True friendship in action. Not just lip-service.

"Caroline, you're home. Let's get in," Catherine said.

The weather was cold with snow still around. As I looked at my house, I said to myself, "Thank God, I'm home again."

When I opened the door, the house was dark without a sound. I was about to turn on the lights when, all of a sudden, the lights were on and my close friends were already there, shouting loudly, "*Welcome home, Caroline. Be healthy and strong!*"

Alice, Helena, Joanna, and Polina were there. Alice even bro-ught a cake.

We really had a party, chitchatting and laughing. They were surprised that I bought each of them a present from Hong Kong. It was a party celebrating the regaining of my health.

"Let's sing the song, *We Shall Overcome,* together, OK?" I led this Ensemble as if I were the conductor of the Vienna Boys' Choir:

We shall overcome,
We shall overcome,
We shall overcome someday,

Oh deep, in our hearts,
We do believe, that
We shall overcome someday.

Yes, we all have to overcome obstacles in our lives. And for me, I have to overcome this mental illness of mine. I knew that in time, step by step, I would be able to overcome my manic-depression and lead a fulfilling life without fears.

"Take your medications, Yeng," reminded my mother again in front of my friends.

"OK, Mom."

This time, I did not lose my temper. Her nagging was her concern for my health. I knew that taking these medications would probably help me stay out of the hospital. And I did not feel embarrassed that she had reminded me in front of my friends. After all, these were a few friends in Toronto who had supported me along the way, though they might not know much about mental illness or understand me as much as my friends in Hong Kong could. They did not desert me, but rather stood by me. They did not judge me or undervalue me because of my illness. Isn't this what good friends are for?

After they had left, it was already three in the morning. I was left alone in my house, looking at the leftover cake.

I will try my best to take my medications, see the doctors, and enjoy my friends' company. I will not be afraid of being sick again, even if I had to be hospitalized one more time. I can no longer live in fear, but rather, in hope for the better.

I will learn to overcome the social stigma by showing to those narrow-minded people that a mentally ill person can function in the world, both in and outside of the home. I am *not* an invalid anymore. Rather, I am a survivor with a deeper insight into my illness. And hopefully, one of these days, God willing, I will be able to help the psychiatrists be more sensitive to the needs of us, the so-called mentally-deranged, whether we

become sick by choice, or by fate.

Once again, home sweet home. The emptiness that I felt in my house with Phillip gone did not exist any more. Right now, this void had been replaced by the support of my close friends, here and in Hong Kong, and the love of my mother, my uncle and my aunt.

I hummed my song, *Home Sweet Home*, alone.

The frosty window, the lamppost on the street, and the maple tree in my front yard will forever be part of the Canada that I have adopted as my new homeland. Yes, Canada, the True North Strong and Free.

Dear God, thank you,
For my safe return to
Canada, my new homeland.

Chapter twenty-five

A Close Call Of Death

It was the end of March, 1999. I was surprised to find myself lying on the bed in the medical ward of Mount Sinai Hospital with a middle-aged lady sitting at the far end of the room. I was also surprised to find an intravenous line connected to my arm and a respirator hooked to my throat. A diaper was wrapped tightly around my bottom. As I looked around the room, there was an old, pale-looking lady in the bed next to me.

Was I in a nursing home? Had I lost control of my bladder? I remembered that earlier, I was in 9 South with my mother. She was, as usual, on her daily visit, bringing me Chinese food. Where was she now? Had she gone home?

The lady came towards me.

"Oh, you're awake now. I'm Mrs. Bailey, the nursing assistant."

I tried to speak, but could not. I could only blink my eyes. What had happened to me? Had I become a mute?

"Oh, poor little thing. I know what you went through. It's tough."

What had I gone through, I wondered.

I pointed at the glass of water that was on the table.

"No, you can't have any water."

"Why?" I whispered again, but my throat hurt.

"No, doctor's orders. You're on an intravenous and a respirator. Come, let me give you a good basin bath."

She went to the washroom and filled the basin with lukewarm water. Gently she undressed me, untied the diaper, and rubbed my body. Had I regressed to infancy? Dignity lost. Pride diminished.

Outside the sky was dark. The room was quiet, except for the moaning of the lady in the other bed. All at once, bits and pieces of what happened came to me.

I was injured in a car accident in Antigua. My brother, my sister-in-law, my mother, and I were on the plane. Suddenly, there was a big commotion and I was out of oxygen. I could hardly breathe, kept yelling in frustration. Yet nobody helped me. Just like what *Psalm Twenty-Three* says,

> *"The Lord is my Shepherd,*
> *I shall lack nothing.*
> *He makes me lie down in green pastures,*
> *He leads me besides quiet waters.*
> *He restores my soul…".*

I found myself in a dark tunnel, peaceful and quiet, with a pool of water around me. Moments later, I was in an open medical tent alone with many of my favorite tropical fruits around me. The nurses and the doctors were too busy to attend to me. The next thing I knew I was lying in a modern, air-conditioned hospital. As if mourning for the dying, my brother, my sister-in-law, and my mother all stood in front of my bed, in silence. They left. I was left alone in the hospital.

Was this a close call of death? Or just a nightmare? I was horrified. Again and again, throughout the night, this fear of death and loneliness haunted me.

I fell into a sound sleep, dreaming of my friends Catherine and Donald in Edward Garden in Toronto, of Chee Man and her children in England, and of Richard reading a French book to me in France.

Confused and lost. Was I in Canada, England or France? There was no clock in the room. Mrs. Bailey was in her morning shift again.

"Come on, sweetie, let me wash your face and give you a mouth wash."

Breakfast came for the lady next to me. Milk, juice, and bagels! I could only look with envy. A nurse came. She changed the dressings on the wound of my throat. Why did I have the wound, I wondered. Was I wounded in the car accident? I did not have the energy to ask.

Catherine and Donald walked into the room. Like a shipwreck ed sailor, I was delighted to see my rescuers.

"Where am I?" I whispered.

"You're right here in Toronto in Room 1738 at Mount Sinai Hospital," said Catherine.

"Not Antigua?"

"Of course not. You've never left Toronto, believe me."

"Car accident?"

"No, Caroline. You were in a coma for two weeks here at Mount Sinai."

"Why?"

Catherine did not answer. Had I contacted Legionnaire Disease as Richard had years ago? He had also suffered from a coma. But I was diagnosed as a manic-depressive. What could have caused my coma though? An over-dosage of the neuroleptic medications? Yes, all at once, I remembered now.

It was November, 1998. I still could not go back to work. It was frustrating. Winter would be coming soon. The thought of staying at home in the winter reminded me of the days when I was released from North York General Hospital in 1980, the days when my relationship with Wilbert was rocky. Yes, same as in those days, I was left in social isolation, except for my mother. My mother, who did not understand my situation with the school board, kept calling me at least seven to eight times a day, worrying about my job and my health. She would repeat the same old sentences every day in her monotonous voice.

"How come you still can't go back to work? It has been over a year since you were in the hospital."

"Have you been taking your medications?"

"Make sure that you turn off the stove and lock the door."

I had learned not to talk back to her. But her constant worries, with good intent, had become an extra burden to me. How could I tell her that I had been on the long-term disability pension from the school board since last year, that I did not know when I would be able to return to work?

It was raining on November 26. I had not been sleeping for the past few days. I was agitated and restless. Afraid that I might become sick, I signed in at the Grace Hospital on a voluntary basis. I thought that since Grace Hospital is in Scarborough, a suburb outside Toronto, and not easily accessible by bus, I could be away from my mother for a period of time. Then the doctors would be able to solve our problems.

But on December 2, I found myself lying in 9 South of Mount Sinai Hospital again. My mother and Auntie Chiu were there, visiting me, bringing me Chinese food. The psychiatrist, Dr. Vallabhaneni, gave me many neuroleptic medications including lithium, haloperidol, risperidone and epival. On December 18, after my discharge, my legs wobbled, my speech slurred, and my vision blurred. I was not myself at all.

I withdrew from all the medications on my own. This resulted in my hospitalization again in Mount Sinai on February 25, 1999, with Dr. Vallabhaneni as my staff psychiatrist again.

Perphanizane, haloperidol, lithium, epival, clonazapam, and cogentin were given to me. My speech became slurred again, my sleep was uneven, and my visits to the washroom more frequent. Friends who visited me told me that I was already confused and faltered. Unlike my usual self, I became verbally abusive to the nurses.

Dr. Vallabhaneni then further gave me gabapentin and olanzapine after which I became unconscious and had to be rushed to the intensive care unit for two weeks.

"I can't speak. Why?" I asked Catherine.

Hesitant, she looked at Donald.

"You had a tracheotomy," Donald said gently.

"What?"

"A tracheotomy is when the doctor opens your throat to help you breathe."

I was right. I had been on the verge of death. Would there be any brain damage? I was worried. Could not express myself in words, I signaled for a piece of paper and a pencil. I wrote my feelings in Chinese.

"No, you won't die. You're fine now, right?" Catherine consoled me. Seeing her friend on the bed like a living corpse, she had no choice but to comfort me.

At that moment, Dr. Lemke and Dr. Hilderbrand came to the room. They gave me some tasks to do: Draw a picture, draw the hands of the clock, and spell the word "world" backward. All of a sudden, I could not spell this simple word! Had I lost my language skills? I was worried again.

After the doctors had left, my mother came to the room. Her already skinny body looked skinnier than ever. Her face was pale. She probably had not been sleeping for days. When she saw me, she looked apprehensive and appalled. I could not blame her. Seeing her daughter in such physical torment was definitely devastating for her.

Other visitors continued to come. Helena and Ken from my high school; my brother Bill and his wife, Amy, my niece Jenny; my friends Rosita, Alice, Angelina, and Betty; and Wendy, another inmate of 9 South. They all stood there, watching me in silence, as if mourners in a funeral. What else could they have said?

Dr. Wong came to see me that night. He was very concerned and suggested that my respirator be unhooked.

"I thought that you would have gone," he said to me in Chinese.

"What?"

"It means that you would have died. But you live. So you live twice. Not many people can do this," he said. He gave me a comforting smile.

Then he assured me, "Remember our song, *We Shall Overcome*? You have overcome death. Don't worry. You'll be fine."

Faintly I smiled back. The room was silent, except for the snores of my neighbour. I looked at the sky outside. Unlike the night when Dr. Wong took me to Mount Sinai Hospital in 1997, there were a few stars. Oh, stars, give me the courage in my fight against my physical torment now.

"Speak louder, Caroline," said Mrs. Bailey, "say water."

"Water," I whispered.

"Use your muscles. Repeat water again. Louder."

"Water."

"That's it. Good, Caroline."

Everyday, Mrs. Bailey was my speech therapist. Had I not been able to project my voice without any problems in the classroom? What had happened? I was afraid that I would never be able to speak again.

The physiotherapist came.

"Squeeze your left hand and squeeze your right hand. Lift your left leg gently now. That's it. Now your right leg."

"It hurts."

"I know, Caroline. Give her a hand, Mrs. Bailey. Lift her to the wheelchair."

"Am I paralyzed?"

"No, you're not," assured the physiotherapist with a smile.

"Why is it that I can't walk?"

"Because you've been lying on the bed for over two weeks. Your muscles have become weak. We have to build up your muscles again, make them stronger. Then, slowly, you will be able to walk on your own again. Don't worry. Take one step at a time, OK?"

Mrs. Bailey wheeled me to the Imaging Department for a test. Then, she wheeled me to another department for another specialist's appointment. It was exciting to be able to go out to see people, far better than having to face the plain wall in the room. I felt as if I were a VIP on a boat cruise with a special escort. At the same time, I feared that I might become a useless, paralyzed vegetable for the rest of my life.

In Mid-April, I was transferred back to 9 South for more observations. One day, I was in my room alone. As I was going to the washroom, I fell. The physical pain and the psychological trauma left me frustrated. I burst into tears. A few minutes later, another inmate happened to come in, lifted me up, and called the nurse.

After a few days, Nurse Gloria insisted on taking me for a walk.

"Come on, Caroline, you have to practice walking again. Let's go. It's spring and the sun is shining. You've been in the hospital too long," she coaxed me in her cheerful voice. "You have to overcome your fear."

Once we were out on the steps of the hospital, I fell down.

"Oh, it hurts. I won't try walking again."

"You have to, Caroline," Nurse Gloria encouraged me. "See, a little baby can't learn to walk without falling. You're not a baby. Come on, get up and walk."

Yes, I had to overcome my fears. Had I not overcome my fear of being laughed at as Ms. Crazy? And had I not overcome my fear of seeking help in a psychiatric institution?

I mustered up my courage. In spite of the pain, I got up and, with the help of Nurse Gloria, I slowly learned to walk again.

It was April 30. Dr. Lemke and Dr. Hilderbrand gave me an evaluation. As if I were back to my high school days when I had to pass the English oral examination, I nervously sat there, answering the questions and drawing the pictures. Some of the tasks were to give the names of five Prime Ministers in Canada, to read a piece from *Time Magazine*, and to explain the meaning of the piece.

"When was the Cultural Revolution in China?"

I paused. After all, I was not familiar with the history of China.

"1967," I guessed, hoping that it was the right answer.

"Yes, you're right. Now, the last question. Can you spell the word

"world" backward for me?"

"dlrow."

"Correct," said Dr. Lemke.

"What is this evaluation about? To test my IQ?"

"No. It is a mental status test to see if your brain functions well."

"So did I pass? Can I be discharged?"

"Yes, you did. You did not suffer from any apparent brain damage from your coma. Congratulations! But still, to be one hundred percent sure, you've to go through MRI before your discharge."

I was relieved. I passed the test! Ever since I graduated from the university, I had not had this feeling of success and accomplishment for a long time. I was so glad that I knew English. How could the doctors evaluate me if I didn't?

I told the good news to my mother who was sitting nervously on the couch nearby. For once in many days, I saw a smile on her face.

Shortly before I was discharged, Dr. Vallabhaneni showed me a video about electric shock treatment.

"Caroline, do you have a Power of Attorney?"

"Yes, I do."

"I would say that you tell your Power of Attorney to put down electric shock treatment in your Power of Attorney Form."

"Why?" I asked. I was scared of such an invasive treatment. I could still remember the loss of memory that Carmen had suffered from her electric shock treatment. After all, had I not suffered enough from my coma?

"Because it is a treatment for people like you who have had many manic-depressive or depressive episodes."

"*No! I will NEVER have any electric shock treatment! Never!*" Loudly I cried out. There had to be other kinds of treatments for a manic-depressive like myself. In Canada, one can refuse any kind of treatments.

"Well, if you don't have electric shock treatment, you may either have

to go to a nursing home or be institutionalized if you have another relapse."

"This is a threat, Dr. Vallabhaneni," I said to him in tears. "You should consult with Dr. Ronald Ruskin. He is a senior psychiatrist of this hospital and he is the psychiatric consultant for the Toronto District School Board. He knows me well as a teacher."

I ran out of his office in desperation. Nurse Cynthia was surprised. Never had she seen me in such desolate state before.

"What's the matter, Caroline?"

I told her what had happened.

"Don't worry, Caroline. Why don't you just jot a note to Dr. Ruskin?"

She gave me a piece of paper and a pencil. In tears, I wrote a note to Dr. Ruskin that she put in his mailbox.

I then made an appointment to see Dr. Wong. I wanted to know more about the rights of a patient.

"No, you don't have to write down electric shock treatment in your Power of Attorney Form. This is Canada," Dr. Wong agreed.

Relieved, I went back to the nursing station of 9 South. I asked Nurse Ruth for a paper. I jotted a note to Dr. Vallabhaneni.

"Dr. Vallbahaneni: After careful consideration of the matter, I have decided not to put electric shock treatment in my Power of Attorney Form. Caroline."

I was discharged from the hospital in the afternoon of May 11. Like an inmate released from prison, I was delighted to be out alive after three months of captivity. I was happy that I could reclaim my independence once again.

A few pigeons were outside the hospital entrance, looking for some leftover bits from the hot dog stand close by. Like the pigeons, I was a free woman again. A Chinese bird out of her cage! Hurrah!

I could see the bright sunlight shining from the blue sky. Yes, spring

had come to Toronto after a dreary winter. And I started singing the song, *The Morning After:*

> *"There's got to be a morning after,*
> *If we can hold on through the night,*
> *We have a chance to find the sunshine,*
> *Let's keep on looking for the light.*
> *Oh, can't you see the morning after?*
> *It's waiting right outside the storm.*
> *Why don't we cross the bridge together*
> *And find a place that's safe and warm.*
> *There's got to be a morning after,*
> *We're moving closer to the shore,*
> *I know we'll be there tomorrow,*
> *And we'll escape the darkness,*
> *We won't be searching anymore."*

Yes, I had already escaped the darkness of death and had moved to the shore of the living. And I will definitely search for a better shelter, safe and warm, for myself in the days to come.

> *Dear God,*
> *Thank you so much*
> *For giving me back my life.*

Chapter twenty-six

Resurrection

"Thank you, Dr. John Klukach, my psychiatrist at the Centre for Addiction and Mental Health, for nominating me. Thank you, Dr. Paula Ravitz, for transferring me to Dr. Klukach. Thank you to my mental health nurse, Ms. Elizabeth Rutherford, and all my friends who had supported me, in particular, Catherine and Donald Lofthouse. Thank you, Dr. Ruskin, Professor Greig Henderson, Dr. Joseph Wong and Neasa Martin, for writing comments for the jacket of my book, *The Tormented Mind.* Thank you to the Mood Disorders Association of Ontario and Toronto for launching my book.

Last but not least, I wholeheartedly have to say a special thank you to my beloved professor of Yale University and friend, Dr. Richard Selzer, a surgeon-turned-writer, for his encouragement, continuous support, and for his editing of my book. Without his understanding and his belief in me as a writer and an artist, I would not be able to have the courage to come back, as I am doing here tonight. A final message that I hope to convey is that everyone, whether they are psychiatric patients or top-notch professionals, should develop an inner strength to combat social stigma towards mental illness and improve his or her own mental health. I'm sure that with courage and determination, everyone could make his or her dreams become a reality. Merci beaucoup encore une fois."

That was my acceptance speech for the **Courage to Come Back Award** banquet at the Westin Harbour Hotel in May 2001. This Award, an annual Award sponsored by the Centre for Addiction and Mental Health in Toronto, was given to me because of my courage in fighting against the social stigma towards mental illness.

I was on the stage in front of an audience of over nine hundred with dignitaries such as the former Premier of Ontario, Mr. Bob Rae. The television crew was filming me then. My interview was televised on the

big screen at the banquet hall. Standing on the stage relived my younger days when I won first prizes for my prose reading and drama at the Hong Kong Music and Speech Festival. Had I not always wanted to have this moment of glory again in Canada? My dream had finally come true.

That night, I wrote a letter to Richard Selzer, telling him of the event.

Dear Richard:

I wish that you were in Toronto tonight to see me accepting the Award. It was a moment of triumph for me as a woman survivor of colour of the mental health system to give a speech with psychiatrists in the audience. I would never have dreamt of it happening to me had it not been for your encouragement to me as a beginning writer and your concern for me as a person. I will forever be grateful for that.

The words that are inscribed in the Award go like this: "The Courage to Come Back Award recognizes and honours people across Ontario who have displayed courage and determination in the face of adversity. The Award, formed from glass, symbolizes how vulnerable and fragile the human spirit can be. Yet when framed with courage and dignity, it is inspiring in its strength and beauty."

In fact, I have also made up lyrics that are based on the theme song of Cats, Memory, but was too shy or afraid to sing it in my acceptance speech. The psychiatrists may have thought that I was in my "manic" phase again and had to hospitalize me! Anyway, here are the words. You may sing along with it when you like. You may find the words quite uplifting. That's what I think anyway.

My friend, don't you get upset with life,
Never give up the dreams
That you have always yearned for.
'Cause in our lives,
there are always some ups and downs,
Don't you worry about your life.

My friend, just get on with life,
And remember each moment
That is so lovely.
Forget all the sorrows and unhappiness of life,
Let your dreams and hopes come true.
Every moment of our lives,
Should be as fresh as the flowers,
We should be prepared,
Never to give up our hopes,
Of what we've set for in life.

What do you think? Tell me.

I remember what you told me in the Cross-Campus Library at Yale University in 1996 about the asylum in the old days in Troy when the patients were kept in horrible conditions. And your Chinese friend who was the psychiatrist-in-chief there did manage to make the conditions better for the patients. I was shocked to know that, even in the States, situations for the mentally ill were so bad just about fifty years ago.

I must have to count my blessings that I live in Canada in this day and age. Had I lived in Hong Kong, I probably would have ended up living in the mental institution forever because of my outspoken and assertive behaviour, which might be considered "abnormal" by a lot of the mental health workers and my relatives there. (Within the Chinese Community, mental illness is oftentimes considered as a shame, a loss of face to the family.)

I also have to count my blessings that I survived my coma and with no apparent brain damage. Today, I can still type, play my piano and, most importantly, think. But my handwriting has been changed permanently. These days, whenever I write, the movements on my right hand have become slower. And my handwriting has become smaller and illegible. Do you know that my bank has to ask

a person of authority to verify my new signature, that I am the same old Caroline? I had to ask the Reverend of my mother's church to verify it for me. I tried to make a complaint to the College of Physicians and Surgeons about the psychiatrist, Dr. Vallabhenani. I even went to the Review Board of the College about it. As expected, the board wrote to me that no disciplinary action will be taken. Still, to me, it is not a battle lost, but a battle won. At least I had done my best to voice my opinions, right? I used to be very much afraid of psychiatrists and doctors. But defending my case in the Review Board meeting with the psychiatrist and his lawyer sitting next to me was a battle won already. You also suffered from a coma years ago. Has your handwriting changed?

Did I tell you that my article, It's Taken 20 Years to learn to cope as manic-depressive, was published in The Toronto Star in February last year? I was so happy about it, not only because it shows that I can write, but because I can help others through my writings and my experience.

I am still unable to go back to work with the Toronto District School Board. I don't think I ever will with my changed handwriting. Besides, after having been off from teaching for over three years now, it would be stressful for me to adjust back to the routine. You know how easily I could have a relapse with stress. These days, my mother has not been feeling well. She keeps complaining that her buttock hurts. So, oftentimes, I have to take her to see Dr. Wong. Just a few months ago, she had to be in the hospital for three days because of her constipation problems.

But you know, I am now teaching English as a Second Language/ Literacy two hours a week at Across Boundaries, an Ethnoracial Mental Health Centre in the west end of Toronto. I like their holistic approach to the recovery of the clients. My students are mostly immigrant survivors from India, Sri Lanka, the Caribbean, and Africa. They suffer from mainly manic-depression, schizophrenic,

Martha Ocampo,
Director, Across Boundaries

depression, and post-traumatic disorder. I am happy there because I feel that I can contribute back to the society with my experience as an English as a Second Language teacher and as a survivor. Helping my students means helping myself.

Because each of my students is at a different educational level, I cater my teaching to suit their individual needs and their moods. Sometimes, I show them movies, teach them songs, give them puzzles to work on, and have guest speakers talk to them. But most of the time, I bring them magazines and newspapers. Ask them to read the articles, discuss them, and write about them. These days, because the students know me, they have begun asking me for consultations on their diet and even medications.

My colleagues there also accept me. I have made friends there too. One of them is Nandini. She is from India and is the program coordinator. The other is Martha from the Philippines, who is the director of the centre. The students there respect me as a teacher.

It is especially satisfying to see the improvement of some of my students. One student from Jamaica had trouble in spelling and reading when I first had her. But these days, she has been writing poems and reading articles from newspapers. Another student was so shy and timid in the beginning. Now she is able to stand up in front of the class and read her articles out loud. Isn't it nice?

You know, I could go on and on about their accomplishments. Teaching at the centre makes me realize that mental illness can hit anyone, regardless of race, culture, class, or intelligence. One of my students from Africa suffers from schizoaffective disorder. He gradu-

ated from the University of Toronto in the Fine Arts Department and composes poems within seconds. Another student is a talented singer who composed and sang lyrics in our ESL Talent Show.

Believe me, my teaching there has broadened my understanding of mental illnesses and, in particular, my manic-depression.

These days, I spend most of my spare time reading, writing, playing the piano, and learning French. Oh, recently, I have joined a gym that is close to where I live. I used to hate exercises, but it turned out that I like it. I manage to go there at least twice a week. You also go to the gym at the Yale Campus, right? I've also paid a lot of attention to my diet, eating quite a lot of vegetables and fruits.

Do you know that I have not been taking any tranquilizers since last year? It seems to me that it was my intake of those heavy tranquilizers in the eighties that had caused me lose interest in the arts. I was unable to think independently and would just believe in others without raising any doubts. You know that this is not my nature. Now, I am just on a minimum dosage of epival, an anti-convulsant medication, with the function of "preventing" another manic episode.

In fact, after my coma, I have been extremely careful about medications. I've checked the side effects of epival from the Canadian Pharmaceutical Companion Book for pharmacists. I've also learned not to take the words of the psychiatrist completely.

As a result of my book, I have, just like Professor John Nash said in his biography, A Beautiful Mind, safety, freedom, and friends that have helped me to recover. Indeed, my old friends have all accepted me once again and I have gained a deeper insight into mental illness. I have survivors who write me emails to share their experiences after they have read the book. I am able to make new friends who are understanding psychiatrists and social workers. One of them is Dr. Mary Seeman. She was the former Psychiatrist-in-Chief of Mount Sinai and is Professor Emerita at the University of

Toronto. Just like you, she has been so supportive and encouraging of my writing.

My present psychiatrist, Dr. John Klukach, is not like any previous psychiatrists I have had. He is a young graduate and is casually dressed. No ties. He does not intimidate me. But most important of all is that he sees me as a human being and recognizes my creativity.

As a doctor, I'm sure you know that it is very important to have a good rapport with one's students.

And Dr. Wong, too. Though he is my family physician, he has always been supportive of my dreams and me. Unlike some psychiatrists who interpreted my dream of being a writer as "grandiose thoughts", and the fast delivery of my speech as "pressured speech", Dr. Wong always believed in my aspirations and me.

But anyhow, we all have to be in control of our own health to the best of our ability. Don't you agree?

You know what my dreams are? That is, to sharpen my skills as a writer so that I will continue to write stories and articles on immigrants and mental health, to give presentations about mental health in order to lessen the social stigma towards mental illness, and one day, to be recognized as a professional in the field. And of course, to have you to continue to be my good friend. Do you think that these dreams of mine will come true?

Hope to hear from you soon. In the meantime, take care. I will send you the pictures of the award banquet when they are ready. You will find that I have gone back to my slim self and that my skin is not pigmented, as in the days when I was taking lithium.

Best wishes always,

Yours,

Fei-Yeng

About a week later, I received Richard's letter:

My acceptance speech at the Courage to Come Back Awards in 2001

Dear Fei-Yeng:

Congratulations on getting your Courage to Come Back Award. Thank you for telling me about the event. I really like the lyric that you made. You should have sung it at the banquet. I wish that I could have been there, but as you know, I am tied up proofreading my new book here in New Haven.

I'm glad that your book has helped both you and others in so many ways. You seem to have a good support system in Toronto now. I'm also happy that these days you tend to take your health into your own hands and that you've stopped taking your tranquilizers. But watch out for the symptoms. If you find yourself slipping away, consult your doctors right away. Take this advice from me, though I am only a surgeon.

It's nice that you enjoy teaching your students at Across Boundaries. It is very important for one to really enjoy what one is doing. After all, life is short.

I am also pleased that you did try your best to fight for your case, though you did not win. But I'm sure that it will be in the record of that psychiatrist. I like your fighting spirit. Believe in yourself. And never give up.

Sure, I believe that your dreams will come true in the time to come. Just take life one step at a time and enjoy every minute of it. Don't worry. I will forever be your good and loyal friend. I will come up to Toronto to see you if the University of Toronto invites me to give some lectures. Then, I will take you to have dim sum. I promise.

Warmly,

Richard.

I certainly am not Jesus Christ who was resurrected from his tomb on Sabbath Day after his crucifixion.

I am only a psychiatric consumer who has risen above the social stigma cast by society, an immigrant fighter of the mental health system and its treatments, and a survivor of my coma.

From the same bedroom window as 1997, I looked at the sky. It was bluish with white clouds moving by. Ah, there was a swallow sitting on

Toronto Friends celebrating my Award

the lamppost outside. Like this swallow, I am free to sing my own songs of hopes and dreams out loud now. I am no longer locked in the iron

cage of solitary confinement. I have broken the silence and the social isolation. I am able to proclaim to all my friends and neighbors, here and elsewhere: hallelujah, I have risen above the social stigma of mental illness.

Dear God,
Thank you for
Making my dreams come true,
And for answering my prayer.

Epilogue One

At the end of August, 2003, I took the VIA train to Montreal and spent a few days there by myself, celebrating my birthday. Smaller in size than the Grand Central Station in New York City, the Gare Centrale in Montreal is modern and clean with French and English signs and an underground to the subway station.

I stayed at a bed and breakfast in the Plateau area. I had my Montreal smoked meat sandwich in one of the stores on St. Laurent Avenue. I then walked along St. Laurent Avenue, bypassing Sherbrooke Street and St. Catherine Street, all the way to Chinatown. To my surprise, this Chinatown, though designated as a tourist attraction, is smaller than the one in Toronto. The pedestrian-only street, Rue de la Gauchetiere, has many Chinese restaurants and bakeries. A bit further east is Old Montreal and the famed Notre-Dame Basilica with colourful horse wagons at the curb.

The next day, I took the Metro to St. Joseph's Oratory, Mount Royal, the Biodome, and the Botanical Garden. Both St. Joseph's Oratory and Mount Royal offered a marvelous view of Montreal. I felt as if I were in a tropical forest when I was in the Biodome's rainforest section. The Botanical Garden close by has its Chinese Garden that made it seem as if I were in the Summer Palace in Beijing once again. On my birthday, August 26, I had lunch at a French café on Sherbrooke Avenue and then went to the Museum of Fine Arts across the street. The many exhibits in the museum were very impressive and reminded me of the Museum of Modern Art in New York City. I then went down to St. Catherine Street to the Montreal Museum of Contemporary Arts. There I saw the art exhibits and a documentary of Nan Goldin.

Before the show time for *Miss Saigon* that evening, I sat on a bench at the Square of Place Des Arts, just outside the Montreal Museum of Contemporary Arts, and had my pizza.

A young man came over.

"De l'argent, s'il vous plait. Sans foyer."

I looked at him. A pale-looking man in his mid-thirties, with short blonde hair and both of his ears pierced, he was in jeans and a red T-shirt. On his right arm was a love tattoo. On his back was his worn-out sleeping bag.

"Quoi?" I asked in French.

"Change please. I'm homeless," he said in English.

I was surprised to see such a young man homeless.

"Why are you homeless? What's wrong?" Curious, I asked.

"It's a long story," he said as he sat on the bench next to me. "See, I was thirteen when my stepfather molested me. My mother did not believe me when I told her. Afterwards, my relationship with them worsened. I skipped school and started smoking pot. At seventeen, I became attracted to an older man. He was thirty-five. We had a relationship. I became gay. When I told my mother about it, she couldn't take it and refused to accept my behaviour and me. I left home. And have been homeless since."

"Where is your friend now?"

"He died two years ago of an overdose of cocaine."

"Then, how about you? Why don't you go back to school or find a job? You're still young."

"Well, I can't read or write. And with no experience, how can I find a job?"

"Don't you go to the shelters to stay at night? Why on the street?"

"Well, there are lots of regulations at the shelters. I don't like it. I like the freedom of staying on the street."

"You get a welfare check every month. What happens to it?"

"Well, I use it to buy cigarettes and sometimes food."

I knew that he must buy other illegal drugs too. But I did not ask. I gave him two dollars. He said "merci beaucoup" and then left.

This homeless man reminded me of Edmond Yu, a Chinese man afflicted with paranoid schizophrenia, who was shot by the police in

Toronto. I remembered seeing him sitting in front of a church on Dundas Street in Chinatown, wearing a Buddhist robe as if he were a monk. He was quiet and did not annoy the neighbors, except maybe people would cast a look at his odd attire at times. Before he plunged into a downhill spiral as a result of his illness, he was a medical student at the University of Toronto.

In February 1997, a woman called for help at a bus stop. A man had assaulted her. Police came and found Edmond in the bus. He took a little silver hammer out from his pocket, waved at the police, and ignored the policeman's order to stop. The police shot him with two bullets, one to his head, the other to his chest.

I was not at the scene, but his death did raise a lot of controversy about the treatment of the mentally ill. Did the police assume that Edmond was the person who had attacked the woman because of his attire? Did the police shouting at Edmond scare him? Was that what led him take his hammer out in self-defense? Or was Edmond paranoid at the time? Was he hallucinating? Or did Edmond not have a psychiatrist and did not take his medications?

Had there been more understanding of what mental illness is among the general public, Edmond Yu would probably be still alive today.

Whether by choice or by fate, this homeless man and Edmond Yu share the same destiny—outcasts by our society. Yet what caused this man to be homeless? The result of his stepfather's sexual molestation? Was his homosexuality genetic or environmental? There are millions of lost souls in this world who are just like them—victims of abuse, domestic violence, drug addictions, or simply mental illness. For some, their families desert them. But some simply give up their willpower and their hope of leading a more productive life. How can our society help these souls?

I went to the theatre and saw *Miss Saigon*. At the end, Miss Saigon killed herself. Perhaps she was, like the homeless man and Edmond Yu, a victim of circumstances too?

I took the train back to Toronto from Montreal on August 27. While I was on the train, my mind went back to May 2002 when my mother died of bone cancer. She had been sick for a few months. When I took her to the emergency department of Toronto General Hospital on May 22, I sat next to her. In order to ease her pain, I touched her frail hands and sang her favourite song:

"Hark the herald angels sing,
Glory to the new-born king,
Peace on earth, and mercy mild,
God and sinners, reconciled…"

Her arms were hooked to the intravenous. She looked at me, gave me a smile, and started singing in her already fragile voice:

Happy Birthday to you,
Happy Birthday to you,
Happy Birthday to my dear Yeng,
Happy Birthday to you."

Did she know that she was on the verge of death and that she wished me to have a happy life after? I never asked her.

The doctor came and examined her; then, she was wheeled off to her room. I was left alone in the emergency room. Years ago, when I was in the emergency room at Mount Sinai Hospital, I also sang my songs. That was my way of coping with my distress. Yet the psychiatrist, who did not know me, probably had interpreted it as my "manic" behaviour and had me hospitalized. Why was it that now the doctors did not perceive my singing to my mother as "manic"?

As I watched my mother dying in the hospital, my thoughts went back to the days when she was well and without any pain. Ever since I was little, she had been extremely worried about my well-being. She would stay up late if I did not return home on time. And she would insist that Amah Hing take me to school everyday even when

I was in my secondary school years. She did not understand my divorce and became extremely protective of me afterwards. Ever since my father passed away, her worries had indeed become excessive. She would insist that I call her up every night before ten.

Just about a few years before she became sick, she started to remind everyone else, and me in particular, to turn off the stove before leaving the house, to hold on to the keys, to lock the door, and to avoid going to crowded Chinatown for fear of robbery.

She also tended to isolate herself from others, except, of course, me. She preferred to shut herself in her apartment and did not welcome visitors. In spite of my insistence and my brother's, she did not pay much attention to her diet nor her dress either.

Come to think of it, with my new understanding of mental illness, my mother must have suffered from anxiety disorder, obsessive-compulsive disorder, and depression. My psychiatrist confirmed my diagnosis of my mother.

Yet in the past, I did not know much about the symptoms of mental disorders. There were days when I became so frustrated with my mother that I became agitated, guilty, and aggravated in my mood. Had I known more about its symptoms, I would probably have been more understanding and more supportive of my mother. And I would probably have been more at peace with myself.

My mother had to be on the oxygen mask. I knew that her end was near. All at once, somehow, for some unexplained reason, the song, Oh Freedom, which I learned in my high school days, came back to me.

"Oh Freedom, Oh Freedom,
Oh Freedom over me.
And before I'd be a slave,
I'll be buried in my grave,
And go home to my Lord,
And be free."

Yes, in a short while, my mother would be free of all the physical pain and the worldly torments in her life, and be with God in Heaven.

It was night. Outside, the sky was dark. Oh, there were a few stars out there. Perhaps my mother had already found her stars. I silently hummed Beyond The Stars as I looked at her dying body:

"Far beyond the stars, my soul is longing to go,
There beyond the sun, to a better place I know.
Through the darkest night, I can see the heavenly glow,
Far away, beyond the stars.
Time, get you the time, yet is the time so dear,
The bell raising the chime, the morning air is near,
The road leads far away, and soon the day will disappear,
And I'll sing, Hallelujah, and to Him, Hallelujah."

In spite of the stress of my mother's death, I did not have to take any tranquilizers at all. Did it mean that I was in remission? Or I had overcome my manic-depression? Or, perhaps, I knew that the spirit of my mother would forever be with me, that her love for me would never end.

Death is a fact of life. For us, the living, it is the beginning of another chapter of our lives. I am not afraid of death anymore. Was I not on the verge of death in 1999.

Epilogue Two

It was the Tuesday after my trip to Montreal, my usual appointment to see Dr. John Klukach at the Clarke Site of the Centre for Addiction and Mental Health. Amid its low-rise neighbourhood, the building is modern and tall, piercing the sky.

I bypassed the cafeteria and waited for the elevator. Behind the elevator is the emergency room. Had I not once been in this emergency room myself? Yes, I remembered. In 1978, when I faced my marital crisis, the coordinator of the English as a Second Language Department of the Toronto District School Board, Ms. Miriam Diguiseppe, took me to this emergency room. In those days, I did not have any friends at all. The verbal abuse of my ex-husband frightened me. I left home and sought help from my coordinator. She was an extremely caring woman from Yugoslavia who came to Canada when she was very little. Yes, I also remembered that I refused to be an in-patient there. Everyday I stayed in her office, helping her with clerical work. Indeed, I had become a refugee and her office had become my shelter.

As the elevator arrived, out came Dr. Ronald Ruskin. He is a Jewish-Canadian psychiatrist in his mid-fifties who was, at one time, the psychiatric consultant for the Toronto District School Board. After my hospitalization in England in 1992, I had to see him before I could go back to work. I was extremely uptight to see him, knowing that he was the doctor who decides my fate with respect to returning to work.

During the interview, he asked me, "Caroline, have you ever thought of committing suicide?"

His question took me by surprise. In those days, I did not know that people with manic-depression or depression have a high risk of committing suicide.

"Of course not. Why should I, Dr. Ruskin? The world is so interesting and there are so many places that I haven't been to. Besides, there are

so many things that I haven't done."

He looked at me. Then, he asked me another question.

"Caroline, do you hear voices?"

I was shocked again. Again, I did not know that the extreme scenario for a manic-depressive would be to hear voices.

"No, I don't. I am only hearing your voice right now."

Again, my answer probably must have shocked him. He wrote some notes down.

"Dr. Ruskin, I know that you graduated from Queen's University. Afterwards, you went to McGill University, right?"

He was writing his note. He stopped and stared at me, amazed.

"How did you find out?"

"From the Canadian Medical Directory. I knew that the school board must have given you a lot of information about me. So I went to find out about you."

Then, I told him that I was going to read to him one of T. S. Eliot's poems for the simple reason that I was a teacher and it was a good way to check my concentration and my ability to teach. It shocked him too. Probably, he had never had any clients who made such a suggestion to him in the past. Or he had never expected a Chinese teacher to read T. S. Eliot. I read *The Hollow Men*.

Only now do I know that Dr. Ruskin is also interested in literature and that he had studied painting in France himself. These days, he is no longer the psychiatric consultant who has to decide my fate. I find him a compassionate doctor on the humanities side of the profession. In short, he is no longer an "authority" figure to me.

Up to the fifth floor, I waited for Dr. John Klukach outside his office. Again, he is a Jewish-Canadian. But he is a young graduate of about thirty-five from the University of Toronto. Most of the time, he wears jeans. His head is bald and he has an earring in his left ear. He is quite friendly and seems to treat me as an equal. He is not intimidating at all. But still, it took me at least six months before I could trust him and open myself up to him.

"Come on in. I'll be back in a second. Just wait for me, OK?"

I went into his office. To be allowed to sit in a psychiatrist's office without his presence means that he thinks that I am not that "crazy" or "insane." He probably trusts me too.

His office, painted in pale yellow, is nicely decorated with a sofa, a CD player, two end tables, a bookshelf with many books, and a desk with a computer on it. It also has rugs that he brought back from his travels to Morocco and Spain. On the wall are paintings, pictures from Spain, and his diplomas. On the bookshelf is a picture of his two cats. His office has a homey and cozy feeling.

Dr. John Klukach, my psychiatrist, The Centre for Addiction & Mental Health , Toronto

I was looking at one of his books, the DSM-IV Manual, on the shelf when he came in.

"How was your trip to Montreal, Caroline?"

"Wonderful. Had the smoked meat in the restaurant that you told me about. I had a lovely day on my birthday."

"Oh, a belated happy Birthday."

"Thanks. You know, this DSM-IV Manual, the Bible for psychiatrists to arrive at diagnosis, apparently devotes only a small section to the cultural aspect of psychiatry. Don't you agree?" I asked.

"Yes, I do. Do you think that it is necessary?"

"Sure. Sometimes, a person from another culture may have a different way of communicating. For example, I know from my teaching

that when a Sri Lankan woman nods her head sideways, she means yes. If a psychiatrist does not know this, he would have interpreted that she means no. See, psychiatry is, in fact, a science of communication."

I was talking as if I were a professor in Psychiatry, giving a lecture to a resident. Dr. Klukach listened attentively.

"See, I have also been reading some research that says that quite often, African-Americans have been misdiagnosed as schizophrenic because of their different ways of expressing their feelings."

"I agree."

"You know what? Sometimes I wonder if the depression among Chinese may not have been detected right away. Often times, their depression is manifested in somatic symptoms, complaining about headaches and whatnot. And the doctors can't find out the reasons!"

"It's true," said Dr. Klukatch. "Well, Caroline, how's your sleep?"

"Fine. I just take one milligram of ativan on nights when I have problems falling asleep. Last August I experienced emotional turmoil. But I went back to Hong Kong and didn't loose any nights of sleep at all. And no jetlag either. These days, I'm just on a 750 milligram dosage of epival everyday, the anti-convulsant medication that you told me to take. It seems that the prescription of lithium and all those heavy tranquilizers by the psychiatrists in the past did not work for me. It had the opposite effect on me. These days, I am back to my normal self. I'm able to think critically. But the most important thing is that I have regained my confidence and am interested in the arts again."

"That's good. What do you think are the reasons?"

"Well, probably it has to do with my change of attitude to life events. The September 11 attack in 2001 and my coma in 1999 made me realize the unpredictability of life. So why not treasure life and enjoy it to the utmost each and every day? I have tried my best to take my health and my life under control. Besides, most of my dreams have come true. I've also paid more attention to my diet and go to the gym regularly. Oh, I also take Omega-Three Fish Oil. According to a research project by

Harvard Medical School, this natural supplement can help prevent a relapse for manic-depressives."

Dr. Klukach jotted down what I told him in his notepad.

"But I think that my coming to see you regularly does help too. These days, I trust that you would not lock me up unless my behaviour becomes really absurd. You also see that, just like you, I am a human being. For the first time in all my years with psychiatrists, you are one who appreciates my creativity."

"Is that right? It's good that you and I have a good therapeutic alliance."

"I know. Am I not lucky? Thanks to Dr. Paula Ravitz for transferring me to you in July 2000 from Dr. Vallabhaneni at Mount Sinai."

Dr. Klukach smiled. Perhaps he also felt happy that I appreciated him as a psychiatrist.

"But you know whom I should be most grateful for? Richard Selzer, my professor at Yale. Had it not been for his encouragement and his continuous concern for me, I would never have written my book. Then, you would never have nominated me for the Courage To Come Back Award."

"Yes, you should be thankful for his support."

"By the way, I was watching CTV the other day. It says that research in Canada finds that talk therapy can be as effective as tranquilizers and that it can reduce the chance of relapse. See, after my coma, I have been extremely careful with the kind of medications that I take and the dosages. To be honest with you, I went to Shoppers Drug Mart for an information sheet on epival. I found out why I gained so much weight when I was on lithium. That was one of the side effects. Now, I am back to my slim self just as when I was at the university."

"That's good, Caroline, to be knowledgeable of the medications."

"You know that I have been through a lot in the mental health field. I would like to propose some changes to make it better."

"For example?"

"How about having better programs to train the residents? In the area of cultural competence, for instance? Or offering more humanities courses for the residents so that they will be more understanding of the clients' individual needs? Or exposing them to the different kinds of psychiatric treatments from different countries?"

"These are good ideas. I will pass them on to my colleagues. One of these days, we will invite you to be a guest speaker. How about it?"

"I'd love to, with an honorarium, that is. You know very well that I like to give presentations, right?"

"Yes, I know. You have been doing it lately, haven't you?"

"Yes, I have. Oh, I've forgotten to mention that at the end of September, my colleague at *Across Boundaries,* Nandini, another survivor, and I will be giving a presentation at the Making Gains Conference in Niagara Falls."

"What is it about?"

"Well, don't you know? This Conference is organized by the Centre for Addiction and Mental Health and the Canadian Mental Health Association. Our presentation is called Leadership/Advocacy Training for Consumers/Survivors of Colour."

"Oh, it's good that *Across Boundaries* is working on advocacy for immigrant consumers. It blends in with the empowerment of consumers/survivors in the mainstream."

"Sure, it does. That's the purpose of our training program. You know something? I do hope that one of these days, immigrant survivors will be as vocal as survivors in the mainstream. Do you think that it is possible?"

"Why not? If there is a will, there is a way."

Before my forty-five minute session ended, we played one of my favorite songs, *If I Had A Hammer,* from *The Best of Peter, Paul, and Mary* in his CD player.

> *"If I had a hammer, I'd hammer in the morning,*
> *I'd hammer in the evening, all over this land,*
> *I'd hammer out justice, I'd hammer out warning,*
> *I'd hammer out love between my brothers and my sisters,*
> *All over this land…"*

Both Dr. John Klukach and I sang together.

"I do believe in justice and love, don't you?" I asked.

"Yes, I do."

"I also think that there is a fair God too. Perhaps it is God's will that I did not die from my coma in 1999. Had I died then, I would never have had the chance to be actively involved with mental health issues now."

"That's right. There is always a purpose under heaven for everything."

"And I believe in love too. I think that I have also found love now."

"Oh, with who?"

"With my email friend. We have only seen each other very briefly, but throughout our daily emails and letters, I know that love is based on trust, communication, understanding, concerns, and care. Sex is the least important, at least for me. Love should not be controlling or too possessive either. Call my friendship with my friend platonic love, if you want. But I am happy now."

"Good for you, Caroline. Well, it's about time that we should end our session. See you next time."

As I took the elevator down, I ran into Dr. Mary Seeman. She is a renowned scholar in the field of Schizophrenia and is now Professor Emerita at the University of Toronto. She has an office at the centre here. She is very understanding and has been extremely supportive of me.

"Hello, Caroline. Where are you heading?" She asked in her usual kind voice.

"To Chinatown and Harbourfront. And you?"

"To a meeting at the university."

We walked out of the building together. She walked towards St. George Street and I to Spadina Avenue and Dundas Street.

Yes, Spadina Avenue and Dundas Street--this Chinatown where Phillip and I used to go. It has been about six years now. I have not heard from Phillip at all. My memory of him seems to have faded away as time has gone by. Perhaps somewhere in Vancouver, he is happily married and may even have children.

For me, I have also begun a new life. I am not teaching full-time with the Toronto District School Board anymore. Rather, I am working part-time with other immigrant survivors, who, like myself, have survived the mental health system in Canada. I also give presentations to the public to educate them about mental illness. And of course, I am writing this book to bring society's attention to what it is like to go through the mental health system as a psychiatric patient. Hopefully, this book will lead to positive changes in the system itself, sensitize psychiatrists to be careful about diagnoses and treatments, and give the general public better understanding of what mental illness is. Above all, I have to thank God that I survived my coma and am alive today. Each moment of my life, I treasure and enjoy to its fullest.

By the time I reached Harbourfront, it was about six. I sat on a bench facing Lake Ontario. In the distance is Centre Island. When I was in despair, thinking of Phillip, did I not want to have a picnic there once?

Ah, later came the sunset. I could see the sun gradually going down in the purplish red sky above. Was that God's Light? Had He granted His Lights to us, psychiatric patients? Would we be able to hear the voices of our beloved friends and relatives? Were we allowed to love? And would we be accepted and understood?

The gentle waves of Lake Ontario made me think of the turbulent waves in the Victoria Harbour in Hong Kong. I haven't seen Hong Kong for five years now. At times, I do miss the hustle and the bustle of life there. And of course, I miss my long-time girlfriends and my uncle. The quiet and spacious Harbourfront reminded me of Yale University in New Haven. I have not been there since 2001. What does Richard Selzer look like now? Has he aged? After all, I do miss him.

All at once, there was a lone seagull flying above the lake. She was circling around the lake, turned eastward and then went towards the south.

Like this lone seagull, I am still searching for my future direction. Will I stay in Toronto? Or go to Hong Kong? Or to the States? I do not know.

What I do know is that I am no longer a Chinese golden bird locked in an iron cage, singing silently, slowly weeping, *We Shall Overcome.* Instead, like the lone seagull, I am free to fly beyond the barrier of confined isolation, reach out to the bright blue sky, and proclaim to all my friends and neighbours, here and everywhere, "I've *made* it. Rejoice! Hallelujah!"

Dear God,
Thank you once again,
For answering my prayer.
Cher Dieu, merci beaucoup
Encore une fois.

Acknowledgments

I would like to express my gratitude to the following people for their support of the book, in particular, Dr. Mary V. Seeman for her kind editing, Dr. Richard Selzer for his encouragement, and Mr. Jack Pearpoint, my publisher, for his belief in my book.

Charmaine Williams, Assistant Professor, Social Work Dept., U of Toronto

Dr. David Healy, Professor of Psychiatry, Cardiff University, UK

Donald and Catherine Lofthouse

Emiko Kayoma

Geoffrey Reaume, Assistant Professor, Critical Disability Studies, York University. Toronto

Greig Henderson, Associate Professor, English Department, U of Toronto

Jack Pearpoint, Inclusion Press, Toronto

Joanne Campbell, Vice-President, Communications and Public Relations, Centre for Addiction and Mental Health, Toronto.

Dr. John Klukach, staff psychiatrist, Centre for Addiction and Mental Health, Toronto

John Robert Colombo, writer, editor and anthologist, Toronto

Lily Strean

Dr. Mary V. Seeman, Order of Canada, Professor Emerita, Dept. of Psychiatry, University of Toronto

Martha Ocampo, Director, Across Boundaries, Toronto

Nandini Tirumala, Program Coordinator, Across Boundaries, Toronto

Dr. Richard Selzer, Surgeon and writer, Yale University, USA

Dr. Ronald Ruskin, staff psychiatrist, Mount Sinai Hospital, Toronto

Jane Lowry, survivor and writer

Dr. Stanley Sue, Director of Asian American Studies, and Professor of Psychology and Psychiatry, University of California at Davis, USA

Shelia Lacroix, Librarian, Centre for Addiction & Mental Health, Toronto

INCLUSION PRESS ORDER FORM

24 Thome Crescent, Toronto, ON Canada M6H 2S5
Tel: 416-658-5363 Fax: 416-658-5067
E-mail: inclusionpress@inclusion.com WEB: http://www.inclusion.com

Inclusion SPECIAL PACKS... [** = new products]

Item	Price	Copies	Total
All Means All PACK - Video: All Means All, plus & book: All My Life's a Circle	$110 + $10 shipping/pack	____	____
The Community PACK - Members of Each Other & Celebrating the Ordinary - 2 books - John O'Brien & Connie Lyle O'Brien	$ 40 + $7 shipping/pack	____	____
The Education Book PACK - Inclusion: Recent Research & Inclusion: How To - 2 Books - Gary Bunch	$ 40 + $7 shipping/pack	____	____
Friendship PACK (1 book + Video) - [Friendship Video + From Behind the Piano/What's Really Worth Doing]	$ 60 + $10 shipping/pack	____	____
Inclusion Classics Book PACK [Action for Inclusion + Inclusion Papers]	$ 30 + $7 shipping/pack	____	____
Inclusion Classics Videos PACK (DVD format also available) - Videos [With a Little Help from My Friends + Kids Belong Together]	$ 90 + $12 shipping/pack	____	____
PATH IN ACTION PACK (DVD format also available) - 2 Path Training Videos [(Path in Action + Path Training) + Path Workbook]	$150 + $15 shipping/pack	____	____
Petroglyphs Pack - (book & video on inclusion in High Schools from UNH)	$ 60 + $10 shipping/pack	____	____
****PlayFair Teams Kit** - (Teacher's book, Advocate's book , Intro CD, 2 posters)	$ 65 + $10 shipping/pack	____	____
When Spider Webs Unite PACK - Shafik Asante - Book and Video	$ 80 + $10 shipping/pack	____	____

Books

Item	Price	Copies	Total
Action for Inclusion - Classic on Inclusion	$20 + $5 /1st copy shipping	____	____
All My Life's a Circle Expanded Edition- Circles, MAPS & PATH	$20 + $5 /1st copy shipping	____	____
The All Star Company - Team Building by Nick Marsh	$20 + $5 /1st copy shipping	____	____
The Careless Society - John McKnight	$25 + $5 /1st copy shipping	____	____
Celebrating the Ordinary O'Brien, O'Brien & Jacob	$25 + $5 /1st copy shipping	____	____
Circle of Friends by Bob & Martha Perske	$25 + $5 /1st copy shipping	____	____
Community Lost & Found Arthur Lockhart & Michael Clarke	$30 + $5 /1st copy shipping	____	____
Creating Circles of Friends - Colin Newton & Derek Wilson	$25 + $5 /1st copy shipping	____	____
Do You Hear What I Hear? - Janice Fialka & Karen Mikus	$15 + $5 /1st copy shipping	____	____
Dream Catchers & Dolphins Marsha Forest and Jack Pearpoint	$20 + $5 /1st copy shipping	____	____
****Each Belongs** (book with CD) -Jim Hansen w/Leyden, Bunch, Pearpoint	$30 + $5 /1st copy shipping	____	____
****Free to Fly, A Story of Manic Depression** -Caroline Fei-Yeng Kwok	$25+ $5 /1st copy shipping	____	____
From Behind the Piano, by Jack Pearpoint AND **What's Really Worth Doing** by Judith Snow - Now in ONE Book *	$20 + $5 /1st copy shipping	____	____
Hints for Graphic Facilitators by Jack Pearpoint	$25 + $5 /1st copy shipping	____	____
Implementing Person-Centered Planning: Voices of Experience Edited by John O'Brien & Connie Lyle O'Brien	$25 + $5 /1st copy shipping	____	____
The Inclusion Papers - Strategies & Stories	$20 + $5 /1st copy shipping	____	____
Inclusion: How To Essential Classroom Strategies - Gary Bunch	$25+ $5 /1st copy shipping	____	____
Inclusion: Recent Research G. Bunch & A. Valeo	$25 + $5 /1st copy shipping	____	____
It Matters - Lessons from my Son - Janice Fialka	$15 + $5 /1st copy shipping	____	____
Kids, Disabilities Regular Classrooms Gary Bunch	$20 + $5 /1st copy shipping	____	____
Lessons for Inclusion Curriculum Ideas for Inclusion in Elementary Schools	$20 + $5 /1st copy shipping	____	____
A Little Book About Person Centered Planning Forest, Lovett, Mount, Pearpoint, Smull, Snow, and Strully	$20 + $5 /1st copy shipping	____	____
****Make a Difference:** Direct Support Guidebook (J. O'Brien & B. Mount)	$20 + $5 shipping /1st copy	____	____
****Make a Difference:** Leader's Resource Kit (Instructor's book + CD)	$30 + $5 shipping /1st copy	____	____
****Make a Difference:** Learning Journey Booklet (packet of 10)	$20 + $5 shipping /1st set	____	____
Members of Each Other John O'Brien & Connie Lyle O'Brien	$25 + $5 /1st copy shipping	____	____
One Candle Power by Cathy Ludlum & Communitas	$25 + $5 /1st copy shipping	____	____
Path Workbook - 2nd Edition Planning Positive Possible Futures	$20 + $5 /1st copy shipping	____	____
Perske - Pencil Portraits 1971-1990	$30 + $5 /1st copy shipping	____	____
Person-Centred Planning with MAPS & PATH by John O'Brien & Jack Pearpoint	$25 + $5 /1st copy shipping	____	____
Petroglyphs - Inclusion in High School from UNH	$20 + $5 /1st copy shipping	____	____
****PlayFair Teams:** A Manual for Teacher Advisors	$15 + $5 /1st copy shipping	____	____
****PlayFair Teams:** A Community Advocate's Manual	$15 + $5 /1st copy shipping	____	____

Reflections on Inclusive Education — $15 + $5 /1st copy shipping ____ ____

Restorative Justice Art Lockhart, Lynn Zammit, Randy Charboneau — $30 + $5 /1st copy shipping ____ ____

**The Basics-Supporting Learners w/Intellectual Challenge-Bunch — $20 + $5 /1st copy shipping ____ ____

Treasures - from UNH — $20 + $5 /1st copy shipping ____ ____

Waddie Welcome & the Beloved Community T.Kohler & S.Earl — $25 + $5 /1st copy shipping ____ ____

**When People Care Enough to Act (ABCD in Action) — $25 + $5 /1st copy shipping ____ ____

When Spider Webs Unite Community & Inclusion- Shafik Asante — $20 + $5 /1st copy shipping ____ ____

Yes! She Knows She's Here Nicola Schaefer's Book about Kathrine — $20 + $5 /1st copy shipping ____ ____

Inclusion – Exclusion Poster (18 X 24) — $10 + $5 /1st copy shipping ____ ____

Person Centered Direct Support Foldout (call for bulk rates) — $ 5 + $2 /1st copy shipping ____ ____

Inclusion News in Bulk (box of 100) — $50 – includes shipping in NA ____ ____

MEDIA: VIDEOs • CD-ROMs • DVDs

ABCD in Action - DVD Mike Green & Henry Moore & John McKnight (includes book) — $150 + $8 shipping /1st copy ____ ____

All Means All - Inclusion Video Introduction to Circles, MAPS and PATH — $100 + $8 shipping /1st copy ____ ____

Dream Catchers (Dreams & Circles) — $55 + $8 shipping /1st copy ____ ____

Each Belongs (30 years of Inclusion-15 min. celebration in Hamilton) — $50 + $8 shipping /1st copy ____ ____

EVERYONE Has a GIFT John McKnight - Building Communities of Capacity — $75 + $8 shipping /1st copy ____ ____

**Finding Meaning in the Work - (CD + Manual) (O'Briens) — $195 + $8 shipping /1st copy ____ ____

Friendship Video Judith, Marsha & Jack on Friendship — $55 + $8 shipping /1st copy ____ ____

The Inclusion Classics - DVD (2 classic inclusion videos on DVD) — $ 90 + $8 shipping /1st copy ____ ____

Kids Belong Together - MAPS & Circles — $55 + $8 shipping /1st copy ____ ____

The MAPS Collection - DVD (2 MAPS Training videos on DVD) — $150 + $8 shipping /1st copy ____ ____

Miller's MAP - MAPS in Action — $55 + $8 shipping /1st copy ____ ____

**My Life, My Choice - DVD (7 stories of adults with full lives) — $150 + $8 shipping /1st copy ____ ____

NEW MAPS TRAINING Video Shafik's MAP - MAPS Process - Step by Step — $75 + $8 shipping /1st copy ____ ____

The PATH Collection - DVD (2 PATH Training videos on DVD) — $150 + $8 shipping /1st copy ____ ____

PATH Demo Video Univ of Dayton Ohio - Video of Workshop on PATH — $55 + $8 shipping /1st copy ____ ____

PATH IN ACTION Working with Groups -Training Video for Path with Groups — $100 + $8 shipping /1st copy ____ ____

PATH TRAINING Video Intro Training Video - An Individual Path (Joe's Path) — $75 + $8 shipping /1st copy ____ ____

Person Centered Direct Support - CD - 4 minute video & powerpoint — $ 25 + $8 shipping /1st copy ____ ____

Petroglyphs Video Companion to Petroglyphs Book - Packaged with book — $60 + $8 shipping /1st copy ____ ____

**PlayFair Teams DVD an introduction to PlayFair Teams - — $50 + $8 shipping /1st copy ____ ____

ReDiscovering MAPS Charting Your Journey -brand NEW MAPS training video — $100 + $8 shipping /1st copy ____ ____

Together We're Better (3 videos) Staff Development Kit — $175 + $12 shipping ____ ____

TOOLS FOR CHANGE - The CD-Rom for Person Centred Planning ____

Pricing is dependent on a licensing agreement. To obtain licensing information check our website, e-mail or call us.

When Spider Webs Unite - Video Shafik Asante in Action — $75 + $8 /1st copy shipping ____ ____

With a Little Help from My Friends The Classic on Circles & MAPS — $55 + $8 shipping /1st copy ____ ____

Plus applicable taxes (variable)

GRAND TOTAL $==========

Nov. 2006 Listing

Credit Cards on the Net (secure), Cheques, Money Orders, Purchase Orders

• Prices subject to change without notice.
Shipping prices for North America only.
Elsewhere by quote.
* Shipping: Books: $5 for 1st + $2/copy; Videos: $8 for 1st+ $4/copy. OR 15% of total order cost - which ever is less.

New Resources:

- **ABCD in Action**-DVD & Book: **When People Care Enough to Act**
- **My Life My Choice** - DVD - Seven Adults living full lives
- **Make a Difference** - book; training pack, note kit
- **Each Belongs** - book & CD - The 1st Inclusive School Board ever!
- **PlayFair Teams** - 2 books, DVD + Posters - blended teams in schools.
- **Find Meaning in the Work** - CD & Manual - presentation ready!
- **Free to Fly** - A Story of Manic Depression - Caroline Kwok
- **Supporting Learners with Intellectual Challenge** -teacher resources

Tools for Change

CD - Tools for Person Centered Planning

Name: ____________________
Organization: ____________________
Address: ____________________
City: ____________________
Prov/State ____________ Post Code/ZIP ____________
Wk Phone ____________ Cheque Enclosed ____________
Hm Phone ____________ Fax ____________
E-Mail ____________ Web Page: ____________